Cash Flow for Creators

How to Transform Your Art Into a Career

Michael W Lucas

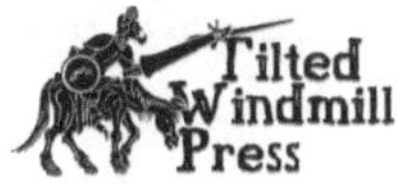

Copyright Information

Cash Flow for Creators

Michael W Lucas

Contents

Acknowledgements

I wrote this book by popular demand, and in self-defense. People kept asking me questions. I want to be helpful, especially to fellow creators. Eventually it was easier to write this book than to explain the topic one more time.

I'm grateful to those folks who read this book before publication and offered useful suggestions for improvement: Misty Bromley, Jamie Ferguson, Barb Giorgi, Bonnie Koenig, Linda Jordan-Eichner, Stefon Mears, Rachel Robinson, Johanna Rothman, Rebecca M. Senese, Mia Tokatlian, Stephannie Tallent, Tami Veldura, and Christina York.

I also vastly appreciate the encouragement and support from everyone in Chicken Club, an author's business and psychiatric support group with a treatable but uncurable fried chicken problem: ZZ Clayborne, Rob Cornell, Brigid Collins, and Alex Kourvo. Despite my last name beginning with something other than that elite bleeding-edge hard "C" sound, they tolerate my presence.

I have an extra bucket of gratitude for Alex, who for several years has reviewed writing how-to books on her Writing Slices blog. She turned her encyclopedic knowledge of the how-to genre and her incisive red pen on an early draft of this manuscript, and helped make this book the best it could be.

Oh, and: Ma Lou's Chicken in Ypsilanti, Michigan. Get some. Just don't get between the writers and their platters.

As always, this is for Liz.

Chapter 1: Creators and Business

You're a creator. You love making a thing. You made the thing, and made more of the thing, and got better at making the thing, until something truly bizarre started happening. The thing became *The Thing*, and people gave you money for it.

Sometimes a lot of money.

And that…is when everything went horribly wrong.

Some of us dream of a day when we can make a living practicing our craft. We look at those who pay the rent by writing books or painting landscapes or hand-carving fountain pens that would make primordial penmaster Walter Sheaffer jealous, and we hunger for that life. Making a living as a creator means being among the best at what you do, so you plunge into study and practice with near monomaniacal focus.

Learn business? Why would you do that, when you could spend that time learning your art? Besides, you've met business people. They're *boring* compared to artistic sorts! And some of the most successful have dollar-store canned chowder for brains. How hard could it be?

Then money appears. And you discover that business is an entirely separate craft. Business is a tabletop role-playing game run by a lackadaisical Dungeon Master who occasionally downs too much caffeine and goes for Total Party Kill. Accepting money for your art shackles you to that game.

Some people realize this, get scared, and stop accepting money. Others don't worry about it until the government tax agents knock on the door and ask if they'll come quietly or would prefer to be dragged. A tragic few of the most skilled artists become so traumatized by business that they flat-out stop practicing their craft.

Some of us deal with the business head-on, and turn the art that brings us joy into our full-time job.

People congratulated me when I started paying the mortgage by writing books. Many folks asked if this was a real thing (yes, it is) and if writers could make money doing it (yes, you can). The question I got most often from my fellow creative sorts, though, surprised me.

"How do you do make a living as an artist?"

Yes, beginners asked. But so did people who were making money at their craft. People who had signed six-figure book contracts or routinely sold paintings for thousands of dollars. They had the skill. They had the market. They had absolutely no idea how to manage what they'd discovered, or how to take that next step.

Making a living with your craft is a long game.[1] Start playing early.

Who Am I?

Who *is* this slick jerk offering to expose the dark secrets of business as a creative for the price of a cheap book? I'm a person with a long and storied history of failure, that's who.

Most businesses fail. The exact numbers vary depending on who you get your statistics from and what they're trying to sell you. Different groups claim that anywhere from twenty to ninety percent of new businesses fail in their first year. Even the optimistic folks that declare eighty percent of all businesses survive their first year admit that seventy percent fail by year ten.

I am no exception. I worked for a bunch of dot-com companies, got tangentially involved with the business side out of self-defense, and watched them fail. I live in Detroit, world capital of Failed Industry Titans and home to thousands

---

1   If this book has a mantra, "art is a long game" is it.

of triumphant small businesses. Watching businesses fail is like reading a magazine's slush pile or judging a student art fair. You learn huge amounts about what *not* to do.

Further, I've run my own failed companies. I failed in publishing in the nineties and consulting in the naughties. Each failure taught me about my strengths and weaknesses. I am a good enough writer that I don't need to do anything but write books. I am a cruel joke of a salesperson. I am imagination-oriented. I am terrible at phone calls. In other words, I'm a tediously stereotypical creative. Any business I run must be oriented to my strengths and must avoid my weaknesses.

I've filed tax returns, dealt with accountants. But most importantly, I've found ways to think about business and money that suit my artistic temperament. My writing business has lasted since the last millennium, and has paid my bills for several years.

Today, I make my living writing books. By *make a living*, I mean I pay the mortgage and an assortment of utilities for my family. By *writing books*, I mean I choose topics that I find interesting and that I think might interest other people, write them, and offer them to the general public.

I don't write for private organizations. I don't consult. I don't podcast, even though my big bald head totally gives me the look of a cheerful supervillain and the thought of *Lex Lucas Against The World* intrigues me. I don't even charge a speaking fee. Should my dulcet rants suddenly be in demand at conferences I might start charging, but only to reduce how frequently I have to find pants and leave the house. I do have affiliate links on my web site; if you follow the links on my site to buy one of my books on Amazon or Kobo or Apple, I get a couple pennies extra. That last covers my gelato bill.[2]

------

2 Don't laugh. It's more than you might think.

I make a living. Writing books. The books I want to write. No excuses, evasions, or elisions.

Could I make more by adding a few hours of consulting, or contracting with a company to produce their documentation, or signing on with a speakers' bureau? Sure!

But I don't want to.

I make enough to live the life I want, save for retirement, and have someone else mow the dang lawn.

Maybe you don't want to go that far. Perhaps you only want to cover expenses, or give yourself a cushion in case of emergency. That's absolutely, 100% valid. But taking money for what you create means you must learn business. More importantly, you must *understand* business. And that's what I'm bringing you. Other books will teach you about double-entry accounting and QuickBooks and ratio of sales to advertising expenditure taxation differentials in multinational whoosamajig please-send-help. I can help you understand what a creative business is, and what it isn't.

I am not an accountant. I am not a lawyer. You should not take anything I say as legal or taxation advice. I live in one city in one country, and you live…probably not here. I can talk about how to manage and interview accountants, but not about specific accounting methods. Find the right support people, like accountants and lawyers and so on. Take their advice. Whatever you do, *be legal*.

The closer your business is to mine, the better my advice will fit you. If you're starting a business that caters to creatives, such as a store or a web site, a book on retail business would help you more than this one. The business of selling beads or journals or paint, while much cooler and more vital than selling mere food and shelter, isn't that much different from any other retail. Reading this book can help you talk with your customers, though, and you should certainly maintain a stock of the paperback at each check-out counter. They're guaranteed steady sellers.

Your Goals

Do you want to make a living at your art and enjoy life? Or do you want to make a couple bucks on the weekend and enjoy life? Something in between? Any choice that ends in *and enjoy life* is perfectly legitimate. Knowing your goals lets you scale your business appropriately.

Goals are not the same thing as dreams. Goals are achievable things that you control. "I will create a new piece of art every week" is a goal. If the goal is reasonable, you can arrange your life to achieve that goal. "My new piece of art will sell for a million bucks" is a dream. It's a great dream. That dream warms your heart as you struggle with your craft up in your unheated artist's garret. With work, your dreams can become goals, and then reality.

Setting up your tiny weekend gig of art sales as an official business will make life easier for you. You have to pay taxes on that income, so you might as well get the advantages too.

Many of us who thought we were making extra money on weekends suddenly found ourselves ejected from the corporate world and plunged into our art as a full-time career. Having the business set up beforehand is a welcome parachute. Start as you mean to go on.

Most of all, set up a business in case you succeed. What if one of your novels or prints or games goes viral, and you're selling thousands of them a day? Random success can destroy people. Having a basic business structure in place beforehand can insulate you and your family from that peril.

Alternately, you can practice the thing you love just for the joy of it and refuse money. That's completely valid. Our culture puts an unholy emphasis on having a "hustle" and not enough on making the best of life, on enjoying what we do, on laughter and love and all the things that fuel our souls. If you keep improving at your craft, though, people will offer you money for it. If you get good enough, they'll keep offering you money. Enough money can tempt the most business-averse person. Set up your business beforehand.

What You Need

Talking business intimidates many creatives. The thought of trawling tax codes, coping with copyrights and trademarks, and quarreling with QuickBooks makes a whole bunch of us nauseous.

I'm not going to make you learn any of that here.

You do need to know how to use spreadsheets. You don't need pivot tables or multi-page references, but you should be able to list items, record the cost of each, and create a total.

Math? You must understand addition, subtraction, multiplication, and division. You have to know that parentheses mean (do this bit first).

I'm assuming that you have basic Internet and computer skills. You can use email and a web browser. You can use a scanner or camera to copy and record paperwork. You can either use a telephone or bribe someone else to make calls for you.

We live in an Internet age. You need a computer nerd who can be easily and inexpensively bribed to tell you how to register a domain name and set up a simple web site. You probably have one in your family. If not, talk to your friends. Computer nerds get incredibly sick of being asked for help, so treat them well. Bribe them, pay them, whatever it takes to make them think well of you and want to aid you. When your business gets big, pay them.

You must back up your business files regularly. A cloud-based backup is okay, provided that the cloud service makes no claim to owning any of the data it backs up. The cloud must be only a backup, though. Original files should remain local, with you, on your computer. Current accounting convention is to save everything to PDF, with copies locally and in the cloud. Cloud-based services have a distressing habit of disappearing overnight, without warning—or, worse, changing their terms of service so that they can sell your data to your competitors. The day your cloud provider disappears with all your records is the day the tax agency sends you an audit notice.

What I Won't Tell You

I'm not going to tell you how to create your art. Your art is not my art. (I will talk about how many professional artists improve their craft, but on a generic level.)

I'm not going to tell you how to *sell* your art. I have no knowledge of the inner workings of any trade except publishing, and that changes so quickly that any book I wrote would become obsolete before I could get it into print. Talk to multiple people in your industry.

I won't recommend specific software solutions. You need a spreadsheet program, but I'm completely indifferent to you using Excel or Numbers or LibreOffice or writing your own spreadsheet program. Your operating system, scanner software, web browser, or email client? If they work for you, they're fine.

I will say that if you use a cloud-based service for anything, carefully study the terms and conditions before using it. Some of those services claim ownership of your files, and not just to support the service you're buying. So long as the service works and doesn't hijack your art, it's acceptable.

Defensive Education

Creative businesses accumulate helpful folks. I hire help all the time. I hire artists, and proofreaders, and too many different kinds of editors. I don't dare do my own taxes.

You need help too. Musicians might hire roadies and studio musicians and sound engineers. We all want to hire the personal assistant who can rub our feet and respond to a raised eyebrow by offering today's delectable dessert assortment.

Once you start making money, though, you'll attract the other sort of help. The sort that's no help at all.

Artists have a reputation for needing business help. Stories from popular culture reinforce this reputation. I don't know how many times I've heard the legend of how Hemingway's publisher bailed him out, or Poe's, or Steinbeck's. The same stories probably circulated about Chaucer. Uncountable urban legends of artists who can't business their way into ordering a meal at the local hamburger joint cement this reputation.

Maybe an artist's publisher or agency took care of the creator, once upon a time.

Those days are *many* decades gone.

People like agents, brokers, and managers might offer to take care of you. They're willing to handle all the messy details of dealing with the business, so you don't have to soil your pristine creative spirit with crass commercial matters. They'll use phrases like "dedicate yourself to your art" and "most people can't understand" and "don't waste your time when you should be creating." Their fees sound modest. They'll present you with easily digested reports and incomprehensible contracts.

I am not saying that all of these people are crooks.

I am saying that scumbags who want to steal from creators take exactly this approach.

It's not that everyone has nasty ulterior motives. Maybe a manager or agent is perfectly honest. But if you don't understand the basics of business, if you can't check your helper's work, you will never know if they're honest or not. The second-greatest financial criminals in history all seemed so trustworthy, until the very end. (The very greatest still seem trustworthy.)

A new saga of violated trust hits every artistic community every month, and every year or so some big-name creator's woes hit the national news. Sometimes predators steal not only money, they steal the intellectual property underlying the creator's craft. I don't want anyone victimized by such predators ever again. Understanding how business works in general, and your business in particular, will help you recognize chicanery and save you both money and heartbreak.

This isn't to warn you off hiring help. I hire artists, editors, accountants, and lawyers the same way I hire plumbers and electricians. I call them when I need them. I pay them a fee appropriate to their labor, and I pay it promptly. I thank them, offer them something to drink, and send them on their way. If my gut tells me they aren't right for me, I don't hire them again.

The difference is, I delegate parts of my business to them. I don't let them direct my business. All monies come directly to me, not to an intermediary like an "agent" or "representative." I (and my family) have the only access to financial accounts. I read and mark up all contracts, then ask a lawyer for help in understanding them.

The only way to protect yourself is to understand what's going on behind the scenes. That means soiling your pristine hands with filthy lucre.

Art, Craft, and Trade

We can all sit around over drinks and debate "But what *is* art? I mean, when you get right down to it?" It's a great game. If we're going to discuss making a living as a creative, though, we must agree what they mean long enough to have the conversation. Here's how I use these terms.

Craft is the nuts and bolts of how you do The Thing. For a writer, it's stuff like grammar and spelling and reading. For a glass artist, it's not mixing different COEs or—at the highest levels—*how* to mix different COEs. Painters need to understand that light and pigments blend colors very differently, how to prep and clean a canvas, and so on.

Art, as a verb, is how you express yourself through your craft. Stephen King and Danielle Steele both work with the same tools of the craft, but they create totally different books. Art illuminates an ideal.

As a noun, *art* is the finished product; the book, the painting, the song, the Thing.

Trade is the business of the finished art. Once you have mastered your craft, you need to master your trade. For writers, it's how to format a manuscript and how to sell your books. For an artist, it's how to get into galleries and garner commissions. Maybe it's how you use Redbubble, Etsy, and eBay. It's how you pay your taxes and siphon off money to pay the mortgage.

Professional artists must master craft, art, and trade.

The Art and Business Hats

The trickiest part about a creator learning their trade?

Never letting the trade into the creative process.

Thoughts like "this will never sell" or, worse, "this will sell millions!" are death to creativity. Create what brings you joy. As a writer I'll spin tales of financial chicanery and betrayal, probably generously leavened with stabbings and shootings and whatnot just to keep my blood flowing. But I can't let considerations of how my business is faring this week get anywhere near my keyboard. An artist should feel free to paint "The Wealthy Give Me All Their Dough" as satirical commentary or plain wish-fulfillment, but shouldn't do "My Dreadful Fiscal Losses This Year, Quarter-By-Quarter, This Is ALL POINTLESS AND I SUCK."

A creator with a stressful job must put aside their concerns to create. You can't fret about your stock portfolio and carve a masterpiece. When you step into your creative space, discard these business concerns in exactly the same way. I promise you that when you finish the day's drawing or writing or sculpting, those concerns will still be there, ready to be picked up. They won't even miss you.

Think of art and business as hats. When you put on the Art Hat, you are purely a creator. You are expressing your innermost self through your craft to create a piece of art. During that moment, you must utterly believe in yourself. Other people have the exact same craft you do. The only thing you own, all you can express, is your sincerity and personal truth. Without letting yourself do that, you have no art.

When you finish your work, take a moment to admire it. Tell yourself you did okay. Creative work is still work, so give yourself a chance to rest.

Then take off the Art Hat, and put on the Business Hat. You've expressed your personal truth, now it's time to trade that work.

Don't even think about the creation process while you're wearing the Business Hat. Don't consider the trade while you're wearing the Art Hat. They must be wholly separate.

Even long-time creators have trouble with this. I just had a discussion with a writer whose artistic side is demanding she write a certain novel. Her business mindset keeps shrieking,

"You don't want to be known for this!" Truth is, her inner creator is going to write the book. The only question is, will she come along quietly or will her Muse drag her by the handcuffs?

Maybe she'll put on the Business Hat afterwards and say "No, this can't go into the trade." That's fine. Everybody occasionally creates unsaleable work. Maybe she'll give it for free to her most dedicated fans, or bury it in the trunk for her literary estate to discover.

My wife, She Who Must Be Obeyed, knitted me a Business Hat and an Art Hat. When I blur the two roles, I literally put on the proper hat and get to work.

"Creators and Business" Action Items

1. What are your goals? A goal is something you control. Making one new piece of art a week is a goal. Writing two books a year is a goal. Buying your own capybara ranch might be a goal, if you have the cash on hand and are ready to call realtors. Write it down: "My goal is…"

2. Perhaps you can't control if your dreams come true, but it's important to admit you have your dreams. What are your dreams for your art? Do you want it to pay the mortgage? Do you want some extra cash? Do you want wealth and fame? Are you looking for a tax break on your fabric habit? Earn heaps of money? Transform your capybara ranch into a capybara dude ranch? Write it down: "My dream is…"

3. Put your written goal somewhere it will regularly remind you to work towards the goal.

4. If you're the sort of person that will be encouraged by seeing your dream, put the dream right next to your goal. If seeing your dream regularly would discourage you, leave it in your notebook. (Admitting it was a dream, and beyond your control, was the important part.)

Chapter 2: Create a Business

Business people have their own language. Corporation. C corp, S corp. Trademark. Limited liability corporation. Initial Public Offering. Sole proprietorship. Copyright, cash flow. Partnership. Non-profit corporation. Trade secrets! Fiduciary! Temple of Mammon! It seems designed to overwhelm. Reading a book on business will explain all of these, but without much context that is useful to you as a creator.

In this chapter, we'll nail down what a business is, its role, and how cash flow figures into it.

What Is A Business?

A *business* is an artificial entity for processing money.

That's it.

Yes, folks with a business degree will stand up here and pontificate about the different sorts of business, and how each has advantages and drawbacks, and how choosing exactly the right sort of business is so vital. They have very legitimate points…but none of that applies to you. Yet.

A business is a bucket to put money in. The business transforms the money into salaries, into fringe benefits, into minimally viable products or infuriated customers or who knows what. The important thing to understand is that a business is an artificial entity that serves your purposes.

This definition of a business applies to a whole bunch of things that we often don't think of as businesses. A household is a business, no matter if it's one person or a nuclear family or a sprawling commune. A family of two adults and a few kids might be born from undying love, but as a household it survives by bringing in money and directing that money to meet its needs. A family that manages money adequately can endure for decades. If it doesn't, well, financial problems implode families just like they do businesses.

Consider the different families you know, and how they run the business of their family. Maybe all the money gets thrown into one pot, and one person is responsible for reading bills and writing checks and balancing accounts. I know some families where each adult keeps their own books, and each person is responsible for certain bills: "I pay the mortgage, you get lights, water, and capybara food." Maybe one person makes and spends all the money, and the other is along for the financial ride.

Businesses have just as much variety, and business people have named each style of financial management. Once you understand that *sole proprietorship* is the same business model as *Mom works and pays all the bills*, it's not so hard. (Yes, Dad legitimately labors by hosing down the kids after school and feeding the capybaras and figuring out what's for dinner, but that doesn't show up on the household ledger except as an absence of housekeepers, chefs, nannies, and ranch hands.)

A business makes decisions in accordance with the business' best interests. The artificial entity borrows a human mind to think. A business' decisions are things like: *should we invest in a new laptop for the artist this year? How much money can we afford to put into retirement accounts? Should we release the new thing this month or in the autumn?* Yes, a human being makes those decisions, but it's not that different from a family. My best interest is in sleeping late on Saturday, but if a family member needs me to take them to an appointment, it's in the best interest of the family that I get up and go.

A business is very different than a family in that you shouldn't get attached to it.

Presumably you formed your family because you kind of like the other folks in it, or at least you're accustomed to having them hanging around. If you have a conflict between your business and your family, always put the family first. You need to take care of your business, but if the current business no longer suits your needs you can reconfigure it, redesign it, or discard it and start over. (The same is true of your art and your craft.) Businesses exist to serve people, not shackle them. Businesses are defined on paper. If you need a second or third business, you can spin them up by filling out forms and paying a fee.[3] You make decisions as the business, but the business exists to serve your needs.

Why Have a Business?

Why can't people just give you money for the thing you love, without you going to the trouble of forming a business? You can do that. Your taxes will go up, but perhaps you really don't want to mess with paperwork.

If you're taking money for your craft, you're in business. Period. The only question is, will you admit it? Will you take advantage of it, or not?

No matter what, you must pay taxes on your income. Evading taxes is a crime. Many governments have upper limits on the amount of income they will ignore. Once you clear that threshold, you must report the income and pay taxes on it. Organizing your creative income as a business simplifies paying those taxes.

An important part of cash flow is knowing where your money comes from. If money appears in your bank account,

---

3   Having a second or third family is not only more difficult, it gets you into all *sorts* of trouble.

is it from your creative work or your salary? Can you afford to quit your job and live off your art? If the money's all in one big heap, there's no way to tell. A business inherently tells you which is which, almost as a side effect.

Governments treat expenditures by certain types of business differently than those by individuals. Your business might be able to pay for tools and supplies tax-free. You can't.

The worst things that can happen to the unprepared creator are financial failure and stratospheric success. If you isolate the financial parts of your craft in a business, you'll perceive impending failure far earlier and have a better shot at correcting course. If your creation goes viral and torrents of money start pouring in, you must immediately contact your accountant and prepare for the deluge. I know more than one creator who went from a couple thousand a year to over a million, with no warning. That lightning strike will change your life. Isolating your creative finances from your personal finances *vastly* eases coping with success. If you're utterly unprepared, dealing with the aftermath of that lightning costs stress, time, and money. Also, the greatest success in the world eventually tapers off. If you isolated your business finances before the lightning hits, you'll recognize normal when it returns.

Fortunately, a business is an artificial entity defined by a piece of paper. You can change that paper.

Naming Your Business

Coming up with a name can be the most annoying part of creating a business. It often seems that the perfect names are already taken. Here's a little secret:

The name of your business doesn't matter.

If you have the perfect name, great! If your name is okay, that's fine.

You have very minor restrictions on your business name. Don't use the same name as a big corporation. Even if your name is McDonald, don't call your art business McDonald's Portraits. It'll draw the attention of the implacable Ronald McDonald, and you don't want to cross that clown—smile or no, he's got more lawyers than you do.

Most difficult, you need a business name that's available as an Internet domain name. People will look for your business name dot com, but if your country has their own top levels like *.au* or *.co.uk* you could use that instead.

If your Muse whispers a name in your ear, great! If not, use the name of the next street over. Or the name of your town with your type of business attached, as in Grimville Publishing or Sugar Valley Sculpture. Or your favorite breed of cow. Or the town with the world's biggest ball of string.

Maybe you can borrow something from a famous book or film. I named my main company Tilted Windmill Press because Don Quixote is something of a role model. When I needed a new company name and "Burke and Hare Press"[4] came to me, the first thing I did was check to see if the domain name *burkeandharepress.com* was available. It was. I bought it. One of the most successful small publishing businesses I know of is named after the initials of the owning family's cats.

The name doesn't matter. Uniqueness and domain name availability does. I mean, what sort of name is "General Motors" for a car company? Who names their new computer company after a piece of fruit? You can even make up a word, so long as it's pronounceable and an Internet search doesn't show it's slang for something nasty.

When you decide which name to register with the government, get your computer geek to help you register the domain name. A dot-com domain name should run you about ten dollars a year. Unless you're an Internet-based business, you

---

4   The three of you who understand the reference may send your hate mail now.

do not yet need email or web hosting or any other service. You only need to stick a flag in the Internet to declare "I claim this chunk of Web for Craft and Country." While you're registering domain names, grab your name dot com if it's available.

Once you have a name, you're ready to create a business.

Stages of a Business

Every business started off as a shmuck with a dream. A fast food franchise might not seem an exciting dream, but despite what the movies say, *I dream of feeding and sheltering my family* is eminently worthy. Our culture overflows with tales of businesses that started in the founder's garage and became multinational gigacorps. I grew up with tales of Henry Ford building the first auto[5] in his backyard shed, and then having to knock out the shed wall so he could get it out. A century later, the Ford Motor Company is an automotive powerhouse despite that early failure of forward planning.

Globe-spanning firms didn't start as big corporations. They started as smaller businesses, and evolved in response to changes in environment. Your business will do the same.

I'm using United States language here. Different countries have other terms for these stages of organization, and manage their licensing and taxation differently. A few countries have unique systems that make sense for more traditional businesses but handicap the small creator. Seek guidance from a local professional creator.

Let's talk about those stages. No matter who you are, start by claiming a business name.

---

5   It wasn't. Not even close.

Business Name

Every country has simple business form of "I'm a person running a tiny business under this name." In the United States this is a *Doing Business As*, or *DBA*. It's often also called "Operating As" or O/A. These are public declarations that you're doing business under an assumed name. "My name is Irette Smith, and I'm doing business as Amazing Arts Atlanta." Most DBAs are filed at a local level, such as a county or parish, and require a modest fee every few years to maintain. It's a toddler among artificial entities. Anyone can go to the county and find out that Amazing Arts Atlanta is you. Legally, it is you.

The chief advantage of a DBA is that it lets you get a bank account under the business name and take payments under that name.

When should you create a DBA? In the United States in 2020, I'd say when you approach four or five hundred dollars a year. That's enough that businesses will soon start sending paperwork with your name on it to tax agencies. Your business bank account prepares you for that moment. If you sold three handmade bracelets last year and made enough for a nice fried chicken dinner and dessert, you probably don't need a DBA yet. Having one earlier won't hurt you. Establishing that bank account early builds good habits and saves you the trouble of changing your bank account in Stripe or PayPal. But you don't *need* it yet.

Any financial benefits or problems with a DBA flow through the business straight to you. A DBA can't go bankrupt; *you* go bankrupt. The DBA can't commit tax fraud, that's all on you.

If you handle all your creative business money through the DBA bank account, converting the DBA to a different business structure is a mere matter of paperwork.

A Group of People

You'll often see unrelated people come together in partnerships. They don't need a big corporate structure yet, but they're going to jointly own a shop or factory. The people don't need a complicated corporation either, but they want to fairly divide the income and losses. Here in the United States, this is called a *Limited Liability Company* or *LLC*. It's great for a family business like a store or dry cleaner or restaurant. If a business is an artificial entity for processing money, the LLC is a great engine for dividing money between folks who do not otherwise share a tax return.

The LLC structure is not so useful for a creator. Your art business probably won't own property or hire staff. Any financial or tax issues and benefits flow through the LLC straight into the owners. The LLC's tax paperwork is part of your tax paperwork.

When should you convert your tiny DBA business to an LLC? That's a decision between you and your accountant. Small business accountants love LLCs, because they're so useful to so many non-creative small businesses. Ask questions like *how will using an LLC reduce my taxes? How will this change benefit me?* It's not that an LLC is bad, but for most creators it doesn't grant many advantages.

Corporations

A corporation is an independent entity. Where LLCs and DBAs have strong ties to people, a corporation exists on its own. The corporation has officers that run it, and owners that reap the benefits, but those are not necessarily the same people. A corporation issues an annual report, files its own tax return, and issues tax forms to the owners so they can do their taxes.

A corporation has its own bank accounts. While that account will have a list of people permitted to access it, the bank account is not the property of any person. For a creator, one of a corporation's interesting characteristics is that it can own or license property, including the intellectual property you create.

When should you use a corporation, and what sort of corporation should you use? That's another discussion between you and your accountant. You need the right accountant, however, and a whole bunch of creativity. We'll discuss the possibilities with corporations in Chapter 5 but in general, in the USA, start investigating this somewhere around fifty thousand dollars a year.

The Reality of Business Stages

All this is fine, but really, what should you do now?

First, remember that your formal business organization—DBA, LLC, or corporation—is a tool that exists to serve you and your goals. You can change that tool as needed. Your country changes the law? Roll with it. Change your organization to fit.

As a beginner, start with a DBA. Get that bank account. Create the separate money bucket so you can start to manage cash flow in the next chapter.

Don't dismiss the idea of going bigger, however. If I look at the peak of my profession, I see dozens of writers who use corporations to optimize their lives. Artists do the same. If a creative business is a long-term game, needing a corporation is the highest level of the game. See Chapter 5 for some possibilities there.

Look at the top people practicing your art professionally. It's easiest to see in books, but catalogs and web sites for other types of creators can leak a surprising amount of business information. Dig into the fine print and you'll see statements like "Copyright 2018 Angry Avocado Rising Inc" or "produced under license from Zen Honey Badger." These artists are using corporations. Perhaps the most famous example is

James Patterson, the biggest selling author in the world, who employs his own editors, cover designers, and more, and who uses publishers mostly as printers and distributors.

Business Bank Accounts

A business absolutely must have its own bank account. Any bills the business pays must be paid from the business account. Your personal bills cannot be paid by the business account. Violating this rule will make the tax agencies come after you for comingling of funds. It's a specific crime in some countries.

Here in the United States, most credit unions will let you open a business account for free, requiring only a minimum balance of five or ten dollars. Don't go to a commercial bank and request a business account; your business is not large enough to tolerate their fees. (When your business becomes large, there's no *reason* to tolerate bank fees.)

The bank account creates a money bucket for your creative business. The bucket is the center and focus of cash flow, as we'll see in the next chapter. Eventually, you'll pay all your creative expenses out of this account.

Once you have a bank account, immediately direct all creative income into that account. From this moment on, the outside world should have no idea that your personal bank account exists. If your business has an online component, tell any existing e-commerce platforms to dump payments into this business account. Pay the expenses for your art out of this account.

Business Income and Expenses

Businesses are artificial entities for processing money. You need to segregate your creative business income and expenses from your family's income expenses. Your money breaks up into four categories.

One category is your family's income from straight jobs. Salaries, hourly pay, and so on all goes to your family.

A second category is money spent to support your family. Rent, food, utilities, and season passes to the petting zoo go here.

The third category is income from your art. Royalties, commissions, and sales of your pieces go here.

Finally, there's money spent to support your art. Artists need paint and canvas and brushes and markers and all sorts of things. Writers need a computer, but depending on how we work we might also need editors or artists or researchers. We all need space to work. Many of us must attend conferences or classes. This is all stuff your business should pay for.

What's a business expense, and what's personal? I write books on technology and Internet engineering. That means my home office needs piles of Internet and a flotilla of computers that can only be described as "indecent." These are all business expenses. If an expense can be a legitimate business expense, assume it's so. Trade and craft conferences? Business expense. Business software, like word processors and spreadsheets? Business expense.

Lunch while you're working is personal, as you'd have to eat anyway. Street clothes are not a business expense, even if your employer's dress code demands everyone wear something, anything. This unfair world expects you to use your own money to purchase pants. Work uniforms and artists' smocks are business expenses, though.

Accountants

The accountant's job isn't only to file your taxes. It's to keep you out of trouble with your taxes. Every business needs an accountant. Finding one is your first real problem.

I make this sound easy, don't I? "Just go find one, la de dah!" The truth is, accountants are everywhere. Your business is so small, almost any small business accountant can handle it. Ask your friends and family for recommendations. Check the Internet for reviews on local accountants.

You don't want a big industrial accountant that prepares tax returns *en masse*. You need an accountant that you can build a relationship with, who will understand your business. You might need to change accountants in some future year. An accountant suitable for your $2,000-a-year business isn't the right person for a million-dollar business.

When you find a small accountant that sounds right to you, call them. Ask them how much they'd charge for an initial one-hour consultation on your new business. The amount varies depending on where you live: Detroit rates are much lower than Silicon Valley!

Bookkeepers traditionally do day-to-day activities like recording receipts, but in some countries they can also do small business accounting. Learn the standards in your country. Maybe you'll wind up with a combination of bookkeeper and accountant. When I say "accountant" in this book, mentally substitute the right person for your country.

If at any time an accountant gives you a bad feeling: leave. Cancel. Say "thank you" and hang up. Find a new accountant. Life is too short to hire creeps. Accountants and other freelancers are accustomed to occasionally losing business. And if an accountant, or any other contractor, gets angry with you for changing? That's proof you made the right decision.

The Company Web Site

Now that you have a company, surely you need a web site. Right?

Sort of.

You do need a web site. It must be on your domain name. Don't try to get by with a social media page, like on Facebook. Facebook charges you to expose your site to your fans. Plus, less than half of Americans use Facebook daily. The percentage is lower in other countries. You want to sell your art to the entire world, not merely half of it.

A web designer might charge you big money to create a full-featured web site. When you're first starting, though, your web site only needs a few things. It needs to say "This is the site for artist So-and-So Whatever." It needs to tell people where to find your work. It needs to tell people how to reach you.

Anything else is extra.

You don't need a blog. If you have a blog anyway, you should link to it—or, better still, if it's relevant to your business, move it on your site. You don't need social media, though if you have accounts somewhere you should link to those as well. You don't need your own online shop. Maybe you'll need it one day, but you certainly don't start with it.

Keep your web site small and simple. Only add new features when you must. And don't let anybody sell you more than you need.

Meanwhile, go read about the cash flow game in the next chapter.

"Creating a Business" Action Items

1. Tell the other decision makers in your family that you're investigating setting up your art as a small business, and you'll probably be asking them some strange questions in the next little while.

2. Come up with a few different names for your company, as discussed in *Naming Your Business*.

3. Ask your computer geek to check which of these names are available as dot-com Internet names. (Absence of a web site is *not* a valid test; I own many Internet domains with no web site.)

4. Of the company names with a domain available, rank how much you like each.

5. Research how to register a DBA in your area, as covered in *Doing Business As*. In most places, the county or parish or city handles DBA registrations. Maybe you can even register it online.

6. Register a company name as a DBA. If someone else already registered your preferred name, work down your list until you find a free one. Save the receipt.

7. Bribe your local computer expert to get the domain name for you, as discussed in *Naming Your Business*. Remember, you don't need a web site yet. You only need to claim that piece of Web territory. Save the receipt.

8. As covered in *Business Bank Accounts*, look for a bank that offers no-fee accounts for small business. Try credit unions first. Ask your friends for recommendations.

9. Take your DBA paperwork to the bank. Verify that they won't charge you any fees to keep your account open, or to use your account. Open a bank account in the name of your DBA. Note where the initial money comes from; your pocket, or art sales? Your accountant may want to know.

10. Log into your new business account's Internet banking site.

11. Make a list of all the possible sources of income for your art: commissions, royalties, Patreon, Kickstarter, contracted orders, publishers, distributors, Third World tyrants and First World plutocrats besotted with your unique vision, and so on. Dream big here.

12. Make another list, of all the things you purchase regularly or have already purchased to create your art. Supplies, components, tools go on this list.

13. Make a third list, of all the things you could purchase that would make creating your art easier. Dream real big here. A personal assistant? Subscriptions to trade journals? Attending the very expensive conferences? A car where all four tires are still round?

14. None of these three lists are immediately complete. Keep them at hand for the next few days. When something you missed comes to mind, jot them down.

15. Talk to your family and friends about small business accountants, covered in *Accountants* earlier this chapter. You probably know one or know someone who knows one. Pick one.

16. Ask the accountant how much they charge for an initial consultation on a small business. If the amount seems reasonable for an hour of a professional's time, make an appointment. (If not, investigate other accountants. If they're all changing about the same amount, raise your estimate of how much a professional charges for their time.)

17. Take your three lists to the accountant. Tell them what you're doing. To advise you, they'll probably want to know where your money really comes from. (That Third World tyrant, while a possible income source, probably hasn't sent you any cash yet.) Go over your lists of expenses and potential expenses, and ask which are deductible in your country. Ask them any other questions you have.

Chapter 3: The Cash Flow Game

Business and cash flow are a game. It has simple rules and straightforward goals. I keep calling a business a bucket to put money in, because the Cash Flow Game is called "Fill The Bucket."

Money enters the Bucket irregularly. A painter might get three commission checks one month and nothing the next. An author might get great big checks for their best-selling novels, but those checks arrive only twice a year. Your art might be dominated by a single annual trade show, where you drag home a giant tarp overflowing with hundred dollar bills but make nothing the other three hundred sixty four days of the year. Income streams like Patreon might stay steady for months or years, then skyrocket or plummet. Most creators have no way of predicting exactly how much money will arrive, or when.

Money leaves the Bucket at a more controllable and predictable rate. Imagine a regular water bucket with a hole in the bottom. You can pour water in the top however fast or slow you want, but water leaks through the hole at pretty much the same speed. A hole the size of a pin leaks slowly. A hole the size of your foot quickly empties the Bucket.

Your expenses—rent, art supplies, food, and so on—are the hole in the bottom of the Bucket.

In the beginning, you'll hope that your business can cover its own expenses. You'll occasionally dip into the Bucket to buy a new laptop or a nifty easel or take advantage of a great deal on a metric ton of high-quality clay.

Relying on the business to pay the rent and buy food enlarges the hole in the Bucket. The leak is still pretty constant, but the Bucket empties faster. Your rent won't drop just because your figurines aren't selling, and while you can scrape by on instant ramen you still need to get your prescriptions filled and deal with that adamant ingrown toenail.

Fill The Bucket has three rules.

- When the Bucket fills faster than it empties, you're winning.

- When the Bucket empties faster than it fills, you're losing.

- When the Bucket goes dry, either find more money or you're out of the game.

That's it. That's the entire game. Everything else is fine detail.

The last chapter defined a business as an artificial entity for processing money. For a creator, this entity smooths the irregular bursts of income into a steady stream that pays the bills. You pay the bills each month and check the Bucket's money level. Is it going up? Are you falling behind?

The way money enters and leaves the Bucket is called *cash flow*.

You can be a successful creator and produce top-quality work without playing Fill The Bucket. Professionals are paid, though, and you cannot be a successful *professional* creator without playing the game.

The most successful Fill The Bucket players I know started with tiny buckets. They got paid for a few pieces, filed a DBA, and opened a no-fee business bank account with those initial proceeds. That initial income wouldn't cover their expenses, so they added their own cash as needed. They were going to buy the tools of their craft anyway, they just did it through the business. They learned how money flowed through their trade, the actual cost of their art, and fine-tuned their understanding every time their income increased and circumstances changed.

The best part of starting your creative business early is that you're (hopefully) not depending on that income to eat. You can afford to lose. Make your business mistakes early in your career, before you even think of going full time.

Every successful business plays some variant of this game. The only difference is how complicated the spreadsheets are.

Tax Deductions

Why do so many business folks focus on tax deductions and deductible expenses? Taxes are most often a company's single largest expense. As an independent creator, that's probably true for you. Tax deductions are the easiest way to reduce your biggest bill.

The first problem in tracking The Bucket is learning what is deductible and what is not. I want to offer glib advice such as "if it's an expense necessary for business, it's tax-deductible," but that's not true in every country.

Most countries tax citizens based on income. Tax deductions reduce the amount of income you're taxed on. Suppose your trade brought in $50,000 last year, but you spent $20,000 on tax-deductible supplies, equipment, and trade shows to make that money. You'll pay income taxes on $30,000 of your income.

Not all purchases are fully deductible. An expense that's fifty percent deductible gives you only half the credit of a fully deductible expense. It's still better than paying taxes on the full amount!

Every time you spend money, ask yourself if it's a deductible expense. You'll learn the most common legitimate expenses in a month or two. After a year or two, the question becomes a reflex.

Tracking the Bucket

Different countries have different guidelines on what you can count as business income and what counts as business expenses, so I'm not going to go into detail of what qualifies as each. Wherever you live, there are great big books on what your country considers valid and invalid business expenses. Your local library has them. Consult them when you have questions. Web articles might be okay, but they cannot replace a librarian and fact-checked books.

If you don't want to read those, talk to an accountant. You're going to need one anyway. Paying a small business accountant for an hour of their time to discuss your new business, and which expenses you should track, is a worthy investment. It can also serve as an interview to see if you want to retain this accountant to handle your taxes, which is why it was part of the Action Items in the last chapter.

You're not looking for an accountant who can take you all the way to globe-straddling corporation; you're looking for someone to help you take your first steps. A tricky corporate accountant is not interested in your toddler business.

Your accountant might also recommend a particular tracking tool. These tools simplify preparing your taxes. Accountants love them. Your fledgling business probably doesn't need one, however. I'm a full-time writer, with dozens of income streams, and I still track all my income and expenses with old-fashioned spreadsheets.

Receipts

A receipt is a record that you spent money. The most critical habit for anyone in business is keeping receipts. You must keep the receipt for every last business-related expense. Keeping innumerable tiny scraps of paper printed in fading ink is a nightmare, but most tax agencies (including the IRS) accept scanned copies of paper receipts or emailed receipts instead. Accountants want all receipts as PDF files.

I store my receipts in computer folders by year, with file names that are easily sorted by the year, month, and day of the purchase. The computer can easily sort file names like *2020-02-29 new crayons* into order, showing you all of a single month's expenditures and letting you quickly zoom in on that mysterious entry on your charge card. Putting months or days first in the file name makes sorting impossible.

Remember that all receipts must be legible. Credit card machines use the cheapest possible ink. Scan them as soon as possible.

Maintain a spreadsheet of all business expenses. You'll send it to your accountant at the end of the year.

In addition to saving all business receipts, I save copies of all receipts for household goods, furniture, maintenance, and anything that isn't food. These receipts go into a separate folder, with file names like *2020-01-03 new chairs and super-stabby knives*.

Why bother with this? First, in many countries you can sell assets to your company. When the lamp in my office burst into flame (don't ask), I sold one of my family's lamps to the corporation for half what I paid for it. That moved a few bucks from the company bucket to my personal wallet. The receipt helped establish a base value for that lamp, and the sale reduced the odds of my home office catching fire by nearly a third.

Or suppose my next novel rockets up the best-seller charts and explodes, scattering around it the wreckage of all lesser novels. The company bucket threatens to overflow with the torrents of cash pouring in. It's the dream, right? Here in the United States, you can refile taxes for prior years when circumstances change. Those receipts might help bail me out from a massive tax bill.

Today's most feeble computer can store an effectively infinite number of small business receipts. Establish your most important business habit right off. Keep every receipt.

Invoices

An invoice is a record that someone asked you for money, and why. Keep copies of all invoices as PDF files named after the date, just like receipts.

Invoices are not receipts. Store them separately.

Most of us do not need a spreadsheet for invoices. Your accountant will tell you if you need one. (The magic word is "accrual.")

Income

Most of your income probably appears in your company bank account. I still get paper checks on occasion, but they're comparatively small.

While the bank records all deposits to your account, track your income outside the bank account. You must be able to easily answer questions like "how much money did I make so far this year," and sorting out deposits and transfers in your bank account is an annoyance.

Tracking Spreadsheets

Don't let the word "spreadsheet" intimidate you. A spreadsheet for tracking expenses or invoices needs only three columns. You need an entry to say what the item is. A check from a client? A replacement USB cable for your drawing tablet? A luxuriant custom Model X SUV with all the add-ons for your next book, *Hacking the Tesla for Fun and Profit*? List it with enough detail that you can easily recognize it.

List the date in another column, and the amount in the third.

If you routinely spend money in multiple currencies, add another column for the original price and currency. Track all your expenditures in your native currency.

You need a separate spreadsheet for each calendar year. Save your old spreadsheets.

That's it.

As you gain expertise, your spreadsheet might get more complicated. My spreadsheet has separate tabs for office expenses, software, travel, and so on. I learn about writing from every book I read[6], so every book I purchase is a business expense. Books have their own tab, to keep that voluminous listing from obscuring every other part of my business.

My most important innovation in the spreadsheets, though? Putting the total at the top of the page rather than the bottom. I can see the total immediately upon opening the spreadsheet rather than paging down.

If you feel the need for anything more complicated than this, perhaps it is time to invest in one of those fancy bookkeeping solutions. Any time I feel the urge to look at bookkeeping software, it turns out that I unnecessarily complicated my expense and income tracking. Accumulating complexity is a textbook side effect of me being an absolute geek.

Eventually your accountant might sit you down and says "Look. Buddy. You know you're my favorite client, right? But either you spend the hundred bucks a year for formal accounting software, or I charge you two hundred for coping with your weird spreadsheets." I have not yet hit that point.

The Cost of Your Craft

You love doing the thing. You're going to do it whether you get paid for it or not. You're going to keep your word processor updated or buy art supplies or raw marble or spray paint that *really* sticks to train cars.

When you start thinking about your craft as a business, you need to consider how much all these supplies cost. Maybe

---

6   Some of those books teach me what *not* to do, but still.

you've set a budget to rein in your otherwise insatiable appetite for jewelry findings, or maybe you just buy stuff exactly when you need it. Most of us think we have a good idea of how much we spend, but don't really.

I've known more than one artist who started looking at their craft as a business, kept all their receipts, and discovered at the end of the year that they'd dropped more on their art than on their kids. Many folks are horrified to learn just how much they spent on supplies. The truth is, you've spent that much, more or less, for years. Only your awareness has changed. (If those same kids are hungry and the mortgage company is sending threatening letters, that's another matter!)

The flip side of spending is knowing how many consumable supplies you have. Every art uses supplies. Writers use paper, printer toner, pens, highlighters, paper clips, and so on. I prefer dark purple highlighters. Back in the 1980s, finding a dark purple highlighter was a bigger challenge than finding another quarter for the Pac-Man machine before the timer ran out. I developed the habit of buying every one I saw. I am now the proud owner of several hundred dark purple highlighters, and am forbidden to purchase any more. Knowing that you own more jewelry findings than shown in the Fire Mountain catalog can help dissuade you from buying more. Unless they're *unique* findings, of course.

Knowing how much your craft costs is an essential part of business.

Expenses In The Early Years

You beg, borrow, or hijack the tools you need to turn logs into chainsaw-carved life-sized decorative figures of Snideley Whiplash[7] that would enhance anyone's front yard. You sell

---

7   Don't do this. The Bullwinkle people take intellectual property *seriously*.

those to earn a few hundred bucks. You file a DBA and open that bank account. Congratulations, you are a business!

Then your kid sister shows up and demands that you immediately return her favorite chainsaw. Buying your own totally drains the Bucket.

Let's talk about art versus business for a moment.

I don't write books as a way to make money. I write books because it's part of who I am. When society finally catches on and locks me up in the padded room for the good of everyone, I'll write my tales on the wall of my padded cell in my own dribble. Most every creator feels the same way. That's how we are.

Tax agencies have rules on small business. Those rules change. In my lifetime, I have been told that a small business can lose money for no more than five years, no more than seven years, that it must make a profit of a certain percentage of its income, and a bunch of other rules that I can't be bothered to remember. Remembering the current rules is what accountants are for.

We all know you're going to buy that chainsaw. That paint. Those books.

In the early days of your creative business, the business can't support those expenditures. With time, that will change. When you make five hundred bucks practicing your art and spent six hundred, you might not want to claim all of those expenses.

An accountant is not just someone to fill out your tax forms this year. They should be able to look at your past tax paperwork and tell you that you can't lose money this year or the IRS will declare your business a hobby, or that spending more than five hundred a year on gasoline-powered chainsaws will penalize you under the Uberfluff ruling, or that buying too many logs in two consecutive years automatically triggers an audit. Your accountant should have suggestions on avoiding such traps.

Even if you can't claim all of your craft receipts as business expenses every year, keep those receipts indefinitely. Remember, this is a long game; you might refile this year's taxes five years from now. You're creating because you love it. Take advantage of what's legally available, but don't let the tax agency stop you from practicing your craft.

I spent money learning to write. You spent money learning your art. Deciding that you want to make money with your art doesn't automagically make it profitable. Sometimes, all it does is make your addiction less expensive. Years where you lose money are normal, but strategize with your accountant on how (or if) you should present those losses to the government.

Scooping Money from the Bucket

Eventually your little DBA business makes money. It pays all the expenses of your art, and by some miracle…there's some left over? You have actually made a profit on your art?

Don't rush out and spend it all on new tack for your capybara. Yes, legally speaking, a DBA is you. You can't rob yourself. What many creatives do, however, is blow the profits on capybara tack and not leave enough to pay taxes. Your accountant will advise you on how much to save for taxes. In the absence of information, though, I save at least half of my income after expenses for taxes. If I make $10,000 in a year, but spend $5,000 in expenses, I'm left with $5,000. I save $2,500 for taxes. It's high, but I'd rather be utterly certain I can pay off the tax man than risk federal goons appearing at my door. Err on the side of keeping too much money, and decide how much you can withdraw.

Removing money from your business is called an *owner's disbursement* or *owner's withdrawal*. You own the company. It's your money. Record it on a spreadsheet, then take your capybara to RodentMart and let it pick out its new saddle.

Large swaths of the rest of this book are about spending money.

"The Cash Flow Game" Action Items

1. Do you have a scanner? If not, get one. The cheapest scanner on the market today is almost certainly good enough. If your phone has a good camera, you can probably use a scanner app. Figure out how to use it.

2. Go to your computer. Create a folder for your business. Everything for your business goes in this folder.

3. Create a folder inside your business folder. Call it "Receipts" and the current year, such as *Receipts 2021*.

4. Create a spreadsheet to track this year's expenses. It needs three columns: item, date, and amount. Figure out how to put the total of the "amount" column on the top of the sheet, where you can easily see it.

5. Search your life for craft-related receipts from this year. If you can't find all of your receipts and income records for this year, that's okay. You'll get better.

6. Scan all your paper receipts and put them into PDF files named after the date, such as *2021-03-21 new brushes*. If you have emailed receipts, print them to PDF with the same naming style. Stash all the PDFs in this year's receipt folder.

7. Record each receipt in this year's spreadsheet, along with the date of purchase and the amount. Make sure the "total" entry of the spreadsheet actually shows the total you spent.

8. Create another spreadsheet, for money you've made with your craft. Give it three columns: the source of the money, the date, and the amount. Put the total of the income column at the top of the sheet, where you can easily see it.

9. Search your life for records of money you made. Scan those records or print them to PDF, and record them in your spreadsheet. Again, verify the "total" entry shows the total of your income and not, say, the total of the date column or something.

10. Back up your business folder, both to a flash drive and to some automatic cloud service.

11. Commit to scanning and recording all of your receipts immediately upon purchase.

Chapter 4: The Long Slow Slog

How do you keep creating, while you're trying to build a business on your creations? You need a distinct combination of attitudes to make it as a creative businessperson, a bizarre mix of arrogance and humility and faith and acceptance that many people never manage. Some days I have a whole bunch of trouble with it. Other days, it gives me only a little trouble.

A creative business that makes money but doesn't yet pay all your bills is in the Long Slow Slog. You're making money, just not enough. The Slog might last years. It might last decades. You're not making enough yet.

"Yet." That's the key word. You're still learning how to make money, improving your artistic skills, and figuring out how everything fits together. So long as you continue improving, you will get there.

My Long Slow Slog began when I was eight and a well-meaning uncle made the mistake of paying me a quarter for a story.[8] After decades of work, my business employs me and pays my bills.

The Long Slow Slog is an absolutely critical stage of your career. It's not an easy time. You're still doing some sort of day job to keep the roof over your head and food in your belly. It's also when you learn how the trade (the business of your art) works in the real world.

How do you trudge through this endless era and build a long-term business?

With a support system that includes your family and your attitude.

---

8   I like to think that my incessant follow-up submissions are not what hounded him to his death.

Life and Family

You have other people in your life. You have friends. Maybe a family. Perhaps pets. You have hobbies other than your art. You have a support system with a bunch of pieces.

Keep them.

Working all day and all night every day, without respite, destroys people. You need human contact—if nothing else, the only way to judge your art is by seeing how it bounces off another human being. Creation requires the stimulation of experiencing people and scenery and dogs and even getting stuck behind some cell-phone-babbling cretin driving twenty under the limit in the passing lane. Isolation and monomania mean bad art. Bad art means bad cash flow.

Inspiration is everywhere, but you have to go out into the everywhere to find it. Live your life.

You need your health. The oh-so-romantic tale of the artist who practiced their craft so intensely that they died of diabetes at age 40—but their art shall survive forever? Yeah, that's not so romantic when it's *your* pancreas that's packing it in. Eat well. Exercise. Do the boring things that keep your soul nailed to your body. Poor health leads directly to poor cash flow. If nothing else, do it for the other people in your life. They want you, not your art.

The trick is to arrange your life so you can consistently practice your craft *and* live your life. There was a time in my life where I only had three hours a week to write. I guarded those hours as savagely as a teacup poodle with its very own pork chop. Three hours a week might not sound like much, but one hundred and fifty-six hours a year is a legitimate chunk of time. That was enough for me to write several books and shepherd them through publication. Your art will differ.

Involve your family in these arrangements. Remember that discussion of your family as a business back in Chapter 2?

Reach a schedule that works for everyone in your life. Your art won't always have priority. That's part of living with a family. Accept it.

My wife and I have a rule: only one of us gets to embark on a time-guzzling project at a time. When we were both working for The Man full time, she wanted to get her master's in nursing and become a nurse practitioner. This was a good move for the family. For those two years I published zero books. I still wrote, snatching time here and there, but the family's needs had to come first. When she graduated and my turn came again, I disgorged so many books so quickly it alarmed people. Productive creation is impossible without the support, or at least sincere tolerance, of those around you.

Creative folks tend to obsess about our art. Don't let that obsession overwhelm the importance of your life. Your people will support you much more freely once you demonstrate that they are important and that you not only support them, you do so with a glad heart. When they need you, put them first. They'll pay you back, with interest.

If your family says they support you, but it just isn't working, invest in a few sessions with a marriage or family counselor. This kind of counseling is not about who is right and who is wrong; it is about you and your family learning to settle your own disagreements and come together instead of pulling apart. People who sincerely want their family to function benefit greatly from it. (If one of you is a manipulative jerk, well, that comes out too. Deal with that as you see fit.)

Keep Creating

The Long Slow Slog started because you love The Thing so much that you kept doing it. You improved at it enough that you started to bring in money for it. That made you think that maybe you had a business here. Perhaps you could even make a living with your art.

Whatever you do: *never stop creating.*

Money comes from practicing your art. You must keep making new things. One best-selling book or one perfect painting is not a career.

I know writers who got so wrapped up in selling their books that they stopped writing new books. Painters who made a tidy sum selling prints of a particular painting, and spent the rest of their careers shilling those prints. Public speakers who wrote one fantastic motivational talk and spent the rest of their careers giving that same speech. You become the person who *did*, not the person who *does*.

If your heart says you've said what you had to say, and you're done creating? That's okay. Admit it.

If not, keep practicing.

Deliberate Practice

Think about what happens when you hear your favorite artist is about to release a new thing. You eagerly await its arrival and experience it as soon as possible. After all the anticipation, you're going to have one of three reactions to it.

Every creator hopes their fans will love their new work. As a fan, you *want* to love it. If this happens, great!

You might think it's bad. It happens. Most fans will forgive a creator a goof or an experiment. I'm a huge fan of Samuel L Jackson, Lawrence Block, and The Birthday Massacre, but now and then a movie or a book or an album doesn't work for me. It doesn't stop me from checking out their next one, though. They'd need a string of flops to make me resign from their fandoms.

Or maybe you'll think it's more of the same.

And this—*this*—destroys careers.

People don't want more of the same. They want *the same, only different.* They want the thing they love, plus something extra. They want their creators to achieve new heights, new depths, new *something*. If you want a career, your art must constantly improve.

Without adding new things, your fans will drift away. The cash flow will dry up, and your fans won't be able to tell you why.

The only way to achieve "the same but different" is through practice.

I use the word "practice" in a very specific sense. Creators don't practice like physicians or lawyers. Creators practice more like musicians. They pick a song they want to learn, and try to play it. At first they stumble, but after a few tries they figure it out and can rock a new tune. They then pick a new song.

Deliberate practice focuses on honing one aspect of the art at a time.

Practicing any art requires a collection of skills. Visual artists have to learn about colors and perspective and dozens of other things I don't even pretend to understand. Writing a book isn't about spelling and grammar, it's about storytelling and language and all the little things that let you impose an emotional experience on the reader.

Professional artists constantly improve their skills. That's what makes them professionals and what keeps their audience coming back. Every time I write a book, no matter the genre, I pick a single skill that I'm going to practice. Maybe it's voice or depth or pacing or cliffhangers or a certain kind of emotion. I still have to do all the other things I've previously practiced, but I trust that I know them and they will come when I call. I focus on my target skill.

Visual artists tell me that hands are notoriously difficult to get right. An artist friend decided that her goal one year was to practice hands. She borrowed her friends' hands so she could study and arrange them.[9] She collected and examined photos and paintings of hands. She drew hands every single day, and put bunches of hands in her art. Some worked. Some didn't. Today, other artists gaze upon her hands and writhe with envy.

The hard part about deliberate practice is that sometimes you don't know what you need to practice. Listen to the masters of your art discussing their art. When they mention something you haven't previously thought of, practice it. Perhaps it's a whole new aspect of the art, or a different way of evaluating something you thought you knew. If you can get feedback from practicing professionals, listen to it. If you're truly short on ideas, ask your fellow amateurs.

If you don't improve your skills during the Long Slow Slog, your art will stagnate. People will *not* experience "the same, only different;" they will get only "more of the same." If you constantly practice improving your craft, you will consistently deliver better and better art.

Eventually you'll come full circle. A few years ago, I practiced cliffhangers. I thought I got them down fairly well. Several books later, I realized that my cliffhangers needed more work. It's not that my skill degraded; it's that my skill improved sufficiently that I could *perceive* shortcomings that my last round of practice didn't address.

Don't run your earlier efforts down. Suppose you make something today you think is spectacular. Ten years from now, you should be able to look at it and say, "That's cool. I enjoyed doing that. I can do better now." You did the best you could at the time, and you had fun doing it. What more can anyone ask?

Every time I hear a creator say "I have all the skill I need," I die a little inside. These people are zombie creators. They're done. They just don't know it yet.

------

9   Ask permission before stealing your friends' hands. Don't be rude.

Tracking Your Craft

"Tracking your craft" is a fancy way to say "recording the inventory you create." "Inventory" is a fancy way to say for "stuff your business has for sale." The local Costco has a flock of rotisserie chicken in inventory, while the Sad Party Store at the end of the street has one grungy bottle of Diet Coke that's seen three presidential administrations. Businesses make money by selling inventory. They need to know how much stuff goes in and how much goes out.

How much do you create?

I'm a writer. I wrote four books last year. Easy. How many copies of each book I sold doesn't really matter in this discussion.

If you make something more tangible, like beads or clay figurines or capybara parachutes, your inventory is the number of them you made. If the items are all similar, a simple tally when you finish each piece will start. If you create different types of thing, you'll need a separate column for each type.

You also need to know how much you sell of each thing. The way you track this depends wholly on what you make and how you sell it, so I can't recommend any specific system. Talk to other professionals in your craft. Do what they do.

Also track how much time you spend working on your craft. This isn't only the time you spend actively sewing or writing or working the welding torch. If you have a dedicated workspace that needs cleaning, count that time. I do all my writing on a dedicated computer in my home office. In theory, I can't possibly get dirty or make a mess doing it. Even so, I must swill the filth out of my garret every month or two.

If you decide to go full time, this knowledge will be precious—and there's no other way to get it other than you recording it during the Long Slow Slog.

The Cost of Your Time

Your time has value. The day job pays you for your time, and your trade should pay you for yours. Tracking your craft teaches you how much time you spend creating a thing.

You might discover that you're giving your labor away. If you spend $10 on supplies to make something and sell it for $15, it might sound like five dollars of profit. That doesn't count your labor, though. If you can make ten of them an hour, your labor is $50 an hour. That's real money. If you spend forty hours on each piece, your labor is repaid at twelve and one half cents per hour.

Perhaps that price is all the market will bear, but you still love doing it. At least you know you'll never turn your craft into a full-time job. You might as well run it as a business and get the tax advantages thereof.

Patience

I mentioned someone who practiced drawing and painting hands for an entire year. That's not weird. For a professional creator, this is *normal*. Art as a business is a long game. It absolutely demands patience. If you don't have patience, hurry up and get some.

You've practiced your craft long enough to know that some parts simply cannot be hurried. I write about a thousand words an hour, fifteen hundred under certain circumstances. Nothing except consistent practice increases that speed. I know perfectly well that pushing for three thousand words an hour will ruin the piece. Cool molten glass too quickly and it shatters. Paint needs to dry before you fondle it.

Cash flow and business are not at all different. Pressuring people to buy rather than letting them make up their own mind alienates folks. Glaring at your bank balance and psychically commanding it to swell also does not work, unless you stare long enough that interest appears. That time would be better spent practicing your craft.

But patience is one of those things that's almost impossible to quantify or identify. What does "patience" feel like? How do you act when you're "patient?" I'm not sufficiently self-aware to say "I feel patient." Most of us aren't.

So turn the problem around.

Don't cultivate patience. Eliminate *impatience.*

Impatience is a negative emotion. You make bad decisions under its influence. You can learn to recognize it, and refuse to make decisions when it's present.

Everybody's impatience manifests differently. Maybe it disguises itself as frustration or anger. For me, impatience appears as excessive nervous energy. I burn off that energy through my martial arts practice. After an hour or two of falls and throws and strikes, I don't have the strength to be impatient.

What burns off your impatience? Do that.

Sometimes dealing with impatience is as simple as recognizing the emotion and taking a few deep breaths to clear it away. Completely empty your lungs and get rid of the stale air before that deep breath. I promise you, there's still enough air around for you to have all you want. (If there isn't, quit worrying about your business and deal with the whole "smothering" thing.)

Make all decisions, especially financial decisions, with a clear, patient mind.

How do you know what decisions to make? That's why you learn the trade.

Learning the Trade

When creators who make money from their craft get together, we rarely talk about our creations. Sure, a bunch of authors will spend a few minutes gossiping about the latest Big Publishing Company disaster. We'll take a moment to admire each other's brand-new books, like you do. I'll ask Rob about his flock of beloathed chickens, query Brigid about *that* cat, see what ZZ's discovered this month, and endure Alex's interminable pictures of this month's Guest Dog.

But mostly, we talk about the trade. *Trade* is the business of our art. What's working? What's not?

You want in on these discussions. Most successful creators are generous with their knowledge and are happy to share our experiences. (There are exceptions. Every group has jerks.)

How you join those discussions depends entirely on your art. Maybe your art has conferences. Attend some. If an artist you respect teaches a class, attend it.

This takes years. That's okay. You're in the Long Slow Slog. You're patient.

Listen more than you speak—specifically, listen to the people who are doing the thing you want to do in the way you want to do it. Don't go up to Stephen King and tell him he can't write and that he's running his business wrong. Don't suck up to him either. Even if a creator's work doesn't speak to you, treat them with basic respect. There are big-name writers whose novels I can't stomach, and you know what? They're not bad writers. They are not to my taste, that's all. Many of them are lovely people, and I respect them as artists. I will happily pick up craft and business hints from them.

You need both pride and humility. Yes, you do The Thing. If someone asks, tell them where they can look at your work. Lugging your books or paintings or figurines around the convention with you is crazy tacky.

Respect other human beings above all. That's not just the folks making more money than you. Respect those with less experience than you. Art is full of Cinderella stories, where a nobody suddenly explodes on the scene. Chances are that "nobody" labored on their craft for years before lightning hit them. Do you want the next Hot Thing in your field to remember you as a jerk? Five minute discussions with random people at conferences, about stuff totally unrelated to our shared art, have changed my life—and most often, I didn't even know about it until months or even years later.

Finally, be selective in who you listen to. Some of the people who present well and seem really confident have never succeeded in the field. Never take business advice from someone who was never able to move out of their mother's basement. They can only teach you how to scrape by, and you want to soar. I might ask a dude on his eighth marriage for recommendations on honeymoon destinations, but I would utterly ignore his advice for a long and happy relationship.

Don't accept craft advice from someone who can't yet do the craft. Beginning artists have all kinds of Opinions on How The Art Should Be Done. I had them. You had them. These folks can be your friends. You can support each other emotionally. They can tell you how your art makes them feel, that the credit union down at Fourth and Main offers no-fee business checking accounts, and that the new Star Trek is actually decent. They can't effectively tell you how to improve your art because they don't yet know.

People have long memories. Be sure you're not a bad one.

Using Knowledge

So you've listened to some knowledgeable folks. You've gotten ideas. Maybe you've come up with your own ideas. Don't just run off and try them! Think first. Experiments are vital in both craft and business, but set them up properly.

This is the greatest time in history to have a creative career. While print-on-demand books have revolutionized publishing, we have print-on-demand canvas, board games, and card decks. 3D printers are changing manufacturing. You can make almost anything.

Getting your craft to customers? You can print shipping labels with postage on them at home, and the US Postal Service has flat rate "if it fits it ships" boxes.

Web sites like Patreon and GoFundMe and Amazon and Kickstarter and Etsy have empowered countless artists. Plus, most of the old businesses are still running. If you make physical art, craft shows are more popular than ever. You have more options for shilling your shmutter than any one person can grasp, and you can use any of them you want.

But you can't use *all* of them.

Listen to other people's experiences with different ways of getting your art in front of people. Pay attention to the success stories, sure, but also ask about failures. Failure is far more educational than success, and learning from other people's failures is the best way to get an education. Your life isn't long enough for you to make all those mistakes yourself.

Every one of these tools has advantages and disadvantages. Each of them also works well for different types of people. Crowdfunding is great, for people who have a crowd. Pick tools that fit you, your craft, and your fans.

Once you've picked a few things that might work, figure out what each of them would cost you in both money and time. See what you could do most easily, and try it in a small way. The nice thing is, all these tools require very little commitment. If something doesn't work, or it turns out to be too much of the wrong sort of work, you can stop doing it.

The only way to learn what works for you, and what doesn't, is to try things. The more you experiment, the harder you work, and the more you improve your craft, the shorter the Long Slow Slog will be. It'll still be long, mind you.

If you practice business as well as your creative attitude, The Slog will prove your art could be a full-time career, or not.

"Long Slow Slog" Action Items

1. Discuss with your family setting aside time for your art and your family alike. *Life and Family* covers this. Reaching an agreement with your family will help them enthusiastically support you. When life changes make the plan unworkable, renegotiate.

2. Take a few minutes and ponder why you practice your art. Skip anything to do with money—this is about art, not trade or craft. Write down every reason that comes to mind. Keep the list.

3. Make a list of the skills that make up your craft, as you best understand it. As talked about in *Deliberate Practice*, for every piece you create or every session, pick one to work on.

4. For one week, track how you spend your time in fifteen minute increments. *Tracking Your Craft* talks about this. Don't pick a holiday week or vacation; use what passes as a normal-ish week in your household. How much time do you spend on your art? Are you satisfied with that time? Of the other ways you're spending time, is there anything that's sucking up far more than you thought?[10] Ask yourself if you should stop doing those things in favor of your art?

5. Make a list of different things you can do to learn your trade (the business of your art). *Learning the Trade* has several suggestions. Which can you realistically afford? Which of those seems most likely to give results? Try it.

6. What makes you impatient? What threatens your ability to endure the Long Slow Slog? Reread *Patience*. Think about how you cope with impatience. Write down three things you can do to get rid of impatience. Try them. If they don't work, come up with more. Use the Internet if needed. Keep experimenting until you find something that works for you.

7. What methods of doing business do you use? Which have you heard are useful, but have never tried? As in *Using Knowledge*, pick one of those and investigate what it would take to try it on a small scale.

---

10   Once you find out it's Facebook, swear off the site.

Chapter 5: Mastering the Trade

You have a business. You're preserving every receipt that enters your home. You're selling things. You've talked with the accountant and know if you need to charge sales tax or VAT or bribe customs officials or whatever your country requires. Congratulations! Art is a long game, the business of art is another long game, and you're playing both.

Uh…what now?

Here's the great thing about a baby business.

You can afford to make mistakes.

Business has certain elements in common with visiting the casino. On your first trip to a casino, do you grab your never-before-opened copy of *Poker for Doofuses* and go straight for the thousand-dollar-a-hand no-limit you-are-bankrupt-but-we'll-take-your-spleen-instead games? Or do you find the penny ante section and see how this whole thing works?

In any game, start playing where you can afford to lose.

Learn to play Fill The Bucket at the small stakes table. You're still learning how to extract money from your art. Learning how your Bucket goes empty when an extra fifty bucks will get you back in the game is much better than discovering that when you're paying rent on a five-thousand-square-foot warehouse. This will transform "don't lose money" from something in your head to something in your bones.

What Is Your Craft?

I am a writer. That doesn't mean I put words in a row and get paid for them. I don't sell books, or stories, or articles, or essays.

I *create and license intellectual property*.

If you're the sort of artist that paints pictures, you do the same. The original canvas is one license to your intellectual property. Prints from that original are different expressions of that property. My living room features a print of a painting of mice racing turtles. The print is mine, but the intellectual property belongs to the artist. If I start to sell copies of that print, the original artist will rightfully get upset at my violation of their intellectual property rights.

Public speaking? You wrote a speech. That's your intellectual property. So is your presentation of that speech.

My wife makes jewelry from raw glass stock and sells it at a few different boutiques. My friend Iris makes charming clay figurines and sells them at conventions. Those are intellectual property. Don't think so? Buy one of Iris' figurines, cast it, and start selling knock-offs. Charming or not, she'll come down on you like two tons of lawyers. The lawyers might or might not weigh a total of two tons—but they will be legion, and they will hunger for your tasty hide.

That's not necessarily true for clothing. A knitted hat is deemed a "useful object," and might not be protected by copyright. That's why knock-off fashions are so common. Plushies, figurines, and amigurumis are copyrightable.

Creators create and license intellectual property. Intellectual property is anything you come up with, and how you express it. We have great big bodies of IP law governing how creations of the mind can be licensed, sold, acquired, and managed. Do you need to understand all of the ways? Nope. When your business gets big enough that you need the fine details, get help then. You do need to be *aware* of them, however.

Maybe your creations are by any reasonable standard intellectual property, but the law doesn't grant you that protection. If you knit unique sweaters and sell them, are those intellectual property? They should be, but US law says otherwise. Still, if a big Hollywood star buys one of your sweaters and wears it on the red carpet, demand for your work will skyrocket. (Don't laugh; it happens.) Who could you license your design to? Who could manufacture your sweaters? If you prepare in advance, you might be able to take advantage of the surge.

If you want to become a global force, stop thinking that you make The Thing and consider how you create Intellectual Property. If this is a new idea to you, I encourage you to read Dean Wesley Smith's book *The Magic Bakery*. It's aimed at writers, but the general concepts are applicable to any creative art. If you like podcasts, the archives of *The Creative Penn* has an interview with Smith about the Magic Bakery.

Active versus Passive Income

One key business concept you must understand is active versus passive income. This boils down to a simple question: what must you do to keep the money rolling in?

If you make physical items that you sell, you have *active income*. You must physically make The Thing. Once someone buys The Thing, you must make another Thing to get more money. Selling paintings or figurines or jewelry is active income. Your labor is directly attached to the income.

Passive income means that the money is detached from your labor. Anything that you can sell another of without involving the artist is passive income.

I write books. I don't get paid for the book while I'm writing the book. (Those big mortgage-sustaining publisher advances are history, except in rare cases.) Once the book goes out into the market, bookstores take over. I get paid for the book without performing any further labor. This is passive income. Selling prints of a painting? Album sales? Passive income. (Boxing up prints and albums doesn't count, because anyone can do that.)

Passive income is lovely. If I fall ill and can't work, passive income carries me through. Yes, my income drops when I don't release new books, but if I must choose between *less money* and *zero money*, I'll go with less every time.

When you wear your Business Hat, always consider how you can add passive income streams. Your nifty paintings are active income, but prints are passive. A numbered run of prints are also passive, but they're scarce and so you can charge more for them. If your cover band does live shows, cut an album of the covers that get the best audience reaction.

Even if you think there's no way your art could lead to passive income, watch for opportunities to change that.

Business Expenses

When you work for a company, it's natural to think that the company should pay for everything. Surely the boss wants his company to have a nice office, not this dump? Why is the coffee so terrible, and where did the company find chairs that so thoroughly torment your back?

Owning the business changes your perspective. Cash flow is the life of a business. Spending money affects your cash flow. Intellectually, you already know that spending too much money empties the Bucket and puts you out of business. Most of us don't know it in our bones until we're in the position of managing cash flow.

A small business owner has two rules for spending money.

- If it can be a business expense, it is a business expense

- Spend money on needs, not on wants

These rules are directly contradictory, except when they aren't.

It's A Business Expense

Each and every time a small business owner spends money, she needs to ask herself "Is this a business expense?" If the money's related to your craft, it's a business expense.

You made a list of possible business expenses in Chapter 2. This is not a one-time exercise. Every purchase you make, consider if it belongs on the list.

If you haven't already discussed that list with your accountant, do so. Each country has its own rules on what's an allowable business expense. If something you buy might be an allowable expense, see if it'll work.

Writing technology books is one of my main income sources. This means my home office needs Internet. Not home Internet, where folks browse the web and play games and stream movies. Not even the kind of Internet a hard-core gamer covets. I need enough Internet to choke a hippopotamus. That's a business expense. Anything that goes in your home office is a business expense. If your business takes you to trade shows, you might need a bigger car. Maybe you need a kiln that can handle larger-than-hobbyist quantities of glassware, or special lighting for your paintings. How can you deduct that from your taxes?

Evaluate every expenditure, no matter how minor.

This is a mindset change for many creatives. Buying craft books or clay or yarn or those special purple highlighters is obviously a business expense, but what about the plastic storage bin to put them in? The table and chair you work at? USB cables and replacement keyboards for when your ceaseless pounding-out of manuscript pages cripples the feeble plastic membrane? All of these are business expenses.

Teach yourself to ask this question every time you reach for your wallet.

You'll probably find your expenses increasing with your sales. I found it convenient to have a credit card just for business expenses, and then a separate wallet for that card and related receipts. Your brain is not my brain. Find a method for recording business expenses that works for you.

Creatives absorb inspiration from everywhere and everything. Is this trip for business? Of course it is! Did visiting this new place influence your art? Did you pick up craft tips, or spend an hour drawing pictures of the market square? That weekend you thought was a romantic getaway with your special someone might turn out to spark your next creation. What's the difference between a vacation and a business trip? Can that vacation be organized as a business trip? What would it take to make that happen? Am I visiting the dusty Utah highlands in the heat of summer to dig for fossils, or am I researching a crime thriller that's set in Utah's desolate beauty? I'm not hiking the mountains, I'm discovering how hard it would be to flee through these mountains in July.[11]

A creative's inspiration is her life. You might as well save the receipts and get some tax benefits.

Needs, not Wants

We all have that inner child that, when confronted with something that hits us just right, shrieks "I *need* this!" Part of growing up is teaching that voice that it can't have what it wants. Managing expenses is the flip side of cash flow.

Creatives like nifty things, especially in our field. Painters like paintings. Jewelry makers like jewelry. My relationship with books borders on the indecent, and that's just how it is. I learn more about my craft from every book I read, so they're a business expense. I could claim that my Netflix subscription

---

11 My research showed that fleeing a killer on foot through the Utah mountains in the height of summer would be a very short trip, unless you're dragging a water wagon behind you. The killer doesn't need to even give chase.

teaches storytelling, but I'd probably have to be a filmmaker to get away with it.

When your business is tiny, it can't absorb all of these expenses.

In some countries, overly large deductions will harm your business. Lose money for too many years, and the tax agency might declare your business a hobby. Some agencies throw alarms when you deduct too large a portion of your income. You'll want to ask your accountant how many deductions your country's tax agency will tolerate. Here in the USA, I've heard that spending half your income as expenses is not unreasonable. If you have to spend $5,000 to make $10,000, you clearly come out ahead. If you consistently spend $9,500 to make $10,000, the auditors might wonder why you bother.

If your tax agency places a limit on how many years you can lose money, don't claim all of your expenses. Track them even if you don't claim them. You must know how much your art costs, so that you know what you need to make for it to be profitable. Those receipts might come in useful later, when one of your creations explodes on the market and you need to refile older taxes.

Maintaining the Bucket

The Bucket is the heart of your business. Successful professional creators regularly spend time studying and maintaining the Bucket.

The most frequent maintenance is recording receipts. Most often I scan the receipt the same day I spend the money, but when I have an evening meeting, first thing the next morning is good enough.

Monthly maintenance comes when it's time to pay the credit card bill. I have one credit card dedicated to my business. (It's in my name, but all expenses on that card are for the business.) When the calendar alarm reminds me it's time, I go through the credit card statement line by line. Every item has a receipt, somewhere. I find any missing receipts, document them, and pay the credit card bill.

Yes, it's annoying. Do I have to validate the credit card bill every month? Nope, not at all! I could save those statements until the week before my annual taxes are due and spend a horrific day or two scrutinizing twelve credit card statements, identifying missing receipts, and searching through my email and faded credit card slips in search of proof I paid that expense. It's my business, it's up to me. I will say that finding a missing two week old receipt is *much* easier than unearthing one eleven months old.

Once you record the expenses, go through them. What is your company spending money on? Do you need that? Do you still need that? Are you still paying for some service that you don't use any more? Do you need everything you bought? Maybe there's something you should have bought that would save you money? Do you need that much Internet, that much fuel, that much clay or silver, that many aardvarks?

Only then consider the Bucket as a whole. Is it more or less full than at the beginning of the month? During the Long Slow Slog, increasing the Bucket's balance every month is a victory. You'll have setbacks, sure, but they're temporary.

Perhaps the most important lesson I learned during my Long Slow Slog was that my business would not only have good and bad months. It would have good and bad *years*. If I was to ever make my art my day job, I needed to prepare for economic crashes, pandemics, wars, and other black swan events.

Working for Exposure

People will try to get you to work for free. The most common line they'll feed you is that they "pay in exposure." You cannot buy groceries or medication with exposure. People die of exposure. Never work for exposure. Never. Not even in that special once-in-a-lifetime opportunity. Your work has value. Demand payment.

It is okay for you to choose to work for free. I work for free, for causes and organizations I support. I write pieces for organizations I back, but that's no different than the days I spend maintaining the computer lab at the human trafficking shelter: it's charity. Charity is important. Be charitable.

Businesses that ask you to work for free are parasites. Unlike tapeworms and lice, these parasites must persuade you to accept their infection. They talk a good game. If you accept, they'll return requesting more free work until you say no. Worse, word gets around to the other parasites that you're a willing host. Learn to declare an unapologetic "no." "No" is a complete sentence. You don't need to give a reason. For the notably virulent and insistent parasites, cultivate a special "no" that reeks of ugly low menace. Immediately hanging up the phone when a parasite says "hello" is entirely valid. Filter known parasites' email into the trash. Otherwise, you'll experience The Even Longer And Slower Slog.

There is a type of exposure worth working for. It's the type that both shows off your name *and* comes attached to a payment. If I sell a ten-page piece to a magazine, that piece is a ten page advertisement for my other work. If you paint a mural for City Hall, get paid. In either case, make sure your name is displayed near the piece.

Money and Taxes

The Long Slow Slog is also where you learn how the government taxes your trade, and how to manage money.

Many creators have poor financial literacy. If that's you, I strongly encourage reading a book like *The Millionaire Next Door* (Stanley & Danko, 2010) which teaches several ways to think about money. One of them should work for you. As a small business owner, though, there's one absolutely critical rule: *never spend money until you have it*. Not when you open negotiations to put your glass spikards in a fancy Toronto boutique. Not when you sign the contract. Not when the check arrives in the mail. Do not spend money until the check cashes and the money is safely secured in your account.

You can anticipate spending the money. You can enjoy a fantasy about withdrawing the whole amount in dollar bills and "making it rain," or converting it to nickels and "making it hail." You can make a list of how to spend the money, and spend the wait trimming and prioritizing. But don't put something on the charge card and think you'll pay it off when the cash arrives.

On the flip side, don't buy anything you can't immediately pay for. Putting your business on a credit card and thinking you'll pay it off over time is financial disaster for a company just like for a person.

No matter your trade, you'll find yourself needing to hire help from time to time. Some of that help will come from freelancers or small businesses like yours. Many of them allow you thirty days to pay a bill, as has been the standard for decades now.

Money transfer is nearly instant, though. When it's not, you can take three minutes and have your bank mail a physical check to some voice artist who lives on a tiny wart of land that's barely attached to the far end of Maine.

Independent contractors are pushing to get by just as you are. I *strongly* encourage you to pay them immediately. It's not only kind, it's good business. I've been paying folks as quickly as possible for years. When I need a favor, they remember that I pay quickly and either put me ahead of other clients or squeeze me in somewhere.

Or, you can pay people late. They'll remember that, too.

Taxes are another whole matter, and vary from country to country and from art to art. If you make physical things, you probably have to pay sales tax or deal with wholesale permits. Your accountant knows all about those topics and can tell you when to worry about each. I don't have to worry about that in my trade, but I do have income tax.

The United States federal government taxes income, or how much you make minus how much you spend. The more money you make, the more tax you pay. In the absence of any further information, I save half of my profit for taxes.

I have been known to spend thousands of dollars late in December on tools I seriously need for the next year, simply to reduce my yearly profit and pay less income tax. My publishing empire needed ISBNs, which are fiendishly expensive in the USA. I bought them six months ahead of schedule, in late December.

Unlike contractors, you cannot make friends with a government. Paying taxes early will not ease your future tax burden nor earn you good will. After a few years of paying your business' taxes, you'll have a decent idea of how to estimate this month's or this year's bill.

The part where I said to never spend money you don't have? Don't let taxes become money you don't have. Save money. If I estimate I will owe twelve thousand dollars in taxes, my business saves a thousand dollars a month towards that goal. We'll look at that more the next chapter.

If you're in the United States, I strongly recommend reading the most recent edition of *Tax Savvy for Small Business* from Nolo Press. This book is an absolute compendium of wisdom on how the small business can legally and safely reduce their taxes.

Own Your Career

Nobody but you and your family will take care of you. Friends can help, mentors can encourage, accountants can offer suggestions, but you are responsible for your own career. This responsibility might be annoying, intimidating, or frustrating. But something weird happens when you finally accept it and dig into the problem.

You start making more money.

When you start paying attention to contracts, to where people make their money, to what your trade allows and doesn't allow, you begin to see gaps where money is slipping through your fingers. Seek out people who are practicing your trade, in the way you want to practice it, and ask their advice. I'm a pulp writer, churning out several books a year. An author who releases one book every two years is not a useful model for me.

This is the greatest time in history to be a creator. Almost every artist can manufacture and deliver their work to their audience. Authors can get books in readers' hands without a publisher, artists can sell paintings and prints without a gallery, tabletop game designers can use on-demand manufacturing to slash their up-front investment to levels almost anyone can afford, and if your product can be reduced to bits you are utterly released from the tedious bonds of any physical manufacturing process. Creators can use the Internet to reach customers directly in a way impossible even a decade ago.

I'm not saying that you must do everything yourself. Far from it!

What I am saying is that middlemen, like publishers and galleries and agents and whatnot, must offer you a value that is clearly better than what you can do yourself.

Every art attracts leeches and bad actors. They offer exploitative contracts, do not live up to their promises, and rip off creators. Every art also has a few heroic creators who collect information and expose the crooks. Discover who these heroes are in your trade. Read their web site and sign up for their "Crooks of Our Art" newsletter. Study the abuses of your trade.

Study your contracts before signing them, looking for both those problem terms and ways the other party could abuse the terms. That friendly, delightful person offering you a contract with Big Art Inc? Read the contract with the assumption that once you sign it, you will never hear from that person again. Instead, all of your discussions will be handled by the company's franchisee of Satan. The contract is not there to say how things will happen when everything proceeds happily. It is there to say what you will be granted in exchange for certain rights to your art, and how things will be handled when the process goes badly. Never sign a contract that doesn't explicitly declare how to terminate the contract.

And study your trade.

Figuring Out Costs

One of the vital things you learn during the Long Slow Slog is how much your craft costs. Yes, you added up all your receipts at the beginning, and you've tracked them meticulously ever since. What you haven't done is figured out how much each piece of art costs you to make.

The easy way to estimate costs is to figure out what you need to make The Thing, price those components, and use those to set a price. This method doesn't count your time and is almost certainly incomplete. You can't do a better estimate until you have a couple years of expense data, however.

Suppose I wrote four books last year. My expenses, including Internet connectivity and conferences on writing and publishing and dealing with publishers and printers and editors, totaled eight thousand dollars. In practical terms, each book cost me two thousand dollars to write. If last year Iris spent two thousand dollars on figurine supplies and made two hundred figurines, each figurine cost ten dollars to make.

You could argue that not all of these expenses should accrue to these items. An accountant would certainly say that. Some of your company's expenses are overhead that you must pay just to exist, like heat and lights and water. But the truth is, right now you don't care about the precise cost of each piece. We care about the shape of your business' cash flow.

Iris spends ten bucks on each figurine she makes. If she sells them for ten bucks, she's doing her craft for free. If I sell a book for less than two thousand dollars, I'm losing money.

Remember when I said to track how much time you spent on your craft, including setting up and cleaning up and buying supplies? Divide the number of hours you spend by the number of pieces you created. Are you working for free? You shouldn't be. Your art is worth something.

To learn how to make your art profitable, you must learn the trade.

Could This Be A Full-Time Gig?

You started small and slow. You accumulated experience. You continually improved your art. What does all this give you?

Knowledge and experience. They combine into wisdom.

By learning all of this slowly, and building knowledge and experience, you've grown to understand both your craft and your trade on a deep level. There is no way to know if there's a huge untapped market for high-end capybara parachutes until you offer them to the general public and see what happens. Maybe the market doesn't exist. Maybe the market is huge, so long as the parachutes are in joyful colors.

The Long Slow Slog lets you adjust your prices so that you make a profit—not just a profit on the materials, but to cover the time you spend making each piece. You can hone your craft.

You can investigate different ways of doing trade. You can try weird stuff and see what happens.

Watch your Bucket. Does it grow? If not, you need to charge more. If you can't charge more, then doing what you're doing in the way you're doing it isn't a business. Can you be more efficient in your trade or craft? Where are you spending money that isn't paying off? What can you improve?

Creators and Corporations

Most of us want to be kind, upstanding folks. We want to get along. We want to never hear from the tax agency, avoid lawyers, and pretend that everybody else is playing the same game by the same rules. As your business grows, you'll learn more about business, law, and taxation. If nothing else, talking to your accountant is an education by osmosis. And you'll start internalizing a few facts about modern life.

Many of us are not playing the same game.

There's a portion of any population that looks at any system of rules and says "How can I exploit these rules to my advantage?" They are well aware that *moral* is not the same as *legal*, and that many things that most people consider morally wrong are perfectly legal. Everyone knows that big corporations have lobbied national governments to implement laws to their benefit, and that corporations are not taxed the same as citizens.

What most people don't realize is that these benefits are open to you as well.

If you look through copyright statements on works of art, you'll occasionally see something like ©2015 *The Capybara Corporation* or ©1969 *John Smith Inc.* These creators found it financially advantageous to incorporate and assign their copyrights to their corporation. They used the same laws that the big companies use. Why would they do this? Because the amount they paid in corporate and personal taxes, plus accountant's fees, was much less than the amount they paid for unincorporated taxes.

Most creators don't sell their copyrights to their corporation. They license them instead. It's less permanent, but also less obvious to the rest of us.

A corporation is an independent entity. It is owned by people, yes, but it has its own tax return. It can own property. Would a retreat way off in the woods help you create? The corporation's Board of Directors (that's you and your spouse, or you and a friend you trust and respect, and in certain narrow cases just you) could declare that *it is in the best interests of the corporation that the corporation own a retreat way off in the woods*. Many, many expenditures and deductions pass tax agent scrutiny when you use the magic phrase "in the best interest of the corporation."

So, you create art. You license the art to a corporation, for a fee, under terms that minimize your taxes. You shuffle money around, putting it in places where it gets taxed less. I have more than one writer friend that licenses their work to an S-corp that they own. The S-corp employs a person (the writer) to manage the licensed intellectual property. The S-corp also offers disbursements to the owner. Taken separately, it saves the writer several thousand dollars in taxes.

If you've never worked with corporations, this sounds utterly bogus. How can it be legal? The truth is, every successful corporation does this. Corporate executives don't think it's anything special. I spent decades in the Internet industry, and this setup is dead standard. A programmer on their third or fourth startup who wants to start a company selling their code often opens a corporation and licenses their code to it.

Just because you can, doesn't mean you should. Always stay within your morals. I'm not willing to run my company as an offshore corporation to eliminate certain taxes. Breaking your own moral code is worse for your health, and your creativity, than constantly worrying about money.

What about this "piercing the corporate veil" thing you hear about? That comes into play when the corporation stops paying its debts or commits fraud. Not paying your debts is illegal. Fraud is illegal. Failure to file your corporate paperwork is illegal. Paying your personal mortgage from the company account is both illegal and sloppy—do an owner's disbursement, then pay the mortgage from your personal account. Obey the law. Shuffling money around to minimize your taxes and meet all the bills is a key principle of modern business.

If a person who owns a car wash can do this, so can you.

Every now and then you hear about a creator who gets busted by a national revenue agency for failure to pay taxes. A couple of years ago, a New York Times best-seller worth millions was massively fined for deducting non-permitted expenses. She had followed her peers in buying that luxurious rural retreat to write in, but had not built the business structure that would permit her to do that as a tax deduction.

The hard part of implementing this is to find the right accountant. Most accountants are driven by the goal of "keep the IRS from bothering my clients." This is a worthy goal. You can't use one of these accountants for your creative corporation. You need an accountant who considers the tax code a game to be won. The kind of accountant who doesn't want to be bothered with normal tax returns. They will charge more. They will save you more than they charge.

When your trade starts to bring in more than $50,000 a year, start looking for such an accountant. Pay them for an initial consultation. Talk through your trade, and ask them to consider what could be done. You might not need a corporation yet, but you need to learn when it will become a consideration.

Using a corporation is an advanced form of Fill The Bucket. You wind up with multiple Buckets, each requiring constantly vigilance and regular maintenance. But if the money piles up high enough, you'll save yourself a whole bunch in taxes.

And if the tax agency comes knocking? You have all your receipts. You have remained within the law and your morals. You have followed a professional accountant's advice. In the rare event that you are selected for an in-person audit, don't go yourself; you can and *should* send a representative. People have made a profession out of staring down the tax man, and they're better at it than you ever will be. Your accountant can refer you to one if needed.

You might never get here. But if you improve your craft, practice your art, and study your trade, you just might.

Joy

The Long Slow Slog is where you learn how to work the trade while maintaining joy in your art. You learn what business chores you can do easily, and what drives you mad. A business exists to serve you, not enslave you. You started doing The Thing because you love it. Anything that keeps you from loving it *must* go.

People offer me money to mail them signed books. Sometimes, a lot of money. Dealing with postage and shipping disproportionately stresses me out, however. It drains my joy, so even as a full-time author I don't offer them. Sorry.

If your Bucket is doing well, you might ask those around you for help. I know one writer with PTSD who cannot handle adding up receipts. His spouse handles that for him. I love my sponsors and Patronizers, but loathe packing books to ship to them. I bribe people to help me. (Pizza is *totally* a business expense.)

If it turns out that business isn't for you, then stop doing business. It's okay. Not everything must become a hustle.

Nobody expects you to turn looking at a sunrise or playing with a baby into a for-profit endeavor. Your art can be the same.

"Mastering the Trade" Action Items

1. Creators create intellectual property, as discussed in *What Is Your Craft?* Even if you make something physical, think about the aspects of your art that are intellectual property. Make a list.

2. Reread *Active versus Passive Income*, and consider which sort of income your art generates. Is there a way to add passive income streams to your trade?

3. Revisit your business expenses. Which of these are needs, and which are wants, as discussed in *Business Expenses*?

4. How often do you maintain your Bucket? Weekly? Monthly? The day before taxes are due? What part of Bucket maintenance gives you the most trouble? What makes you want to not study the Bucket? What can you do to make this easier? How can you change your work or your life so that watching the Bucket can become a routine habit? Make a list. One at a time, try them. See what works.

5. Decide how you want to be perceived by people you hire. Do you want to be the sort of person they want to work for? Do you want them to be reluctant to take work from you? As discussed in *Money and Taxes*, if you want them to be eager to work for you, commit to paying people immediately.

6. How do you set aside money for taxes? If you don't have a way to save for taxes, set one up as discussed in *Money and Taxes*. If you would rather experience the adrenaline rush of the last-possible-instant scramble for money to pay the taxes, skip this item.

7. Assume your time has value. As per *Figuring Out Costs*, use your tracked time to figure out how many hours you spent creating your most recent piece of art. How much did you sell it for? How much did you make per hour? Is that enough?

8. Adjust your prices so that you make something on each piece. Play with prices. See what the market will bear.

9. What parts of the trade sap the joy from your life? Do you need those parts? Can you get help with them?

10. What professionals in your art provide blogs, newsletters, or updates on standard contract terms? Sign up for their updates.

11. Everybody has a ritual they perform when they commit to something. Maybe it's a discussion with your spouse, or making it a mantra, or posting it on social media. Perform this ritual to commit to learn your craft, art, and trade, all together, until you achieve your goal. Repeat as necessary.

Chapter 6: Measurements and The Worst Case Scenarios

Being a full-time creator is not about wealth and power. It's about being able to live your life doing the thing you want to do, and maintain that life in the face of personal, national, and even global disaster.

So many folks dream of creating to pay their rent. Remember, a dream is something you don't control. Transforming that dream into a concrete, actionable goal requires knowing how to *get* there. It requires a way to measure success and risk. You must continuously improve your art, understand business, and run your life as if it's a business.

Chapter 4 talks a whole bunch about improving your art, so I won't spend much time on it here. Deliberate practice is the absolute key. Do it, or slowly lose what business you have.

If you have a straight job, you get paid on a semi-predictable basis. You spend money based on what you're paid. Life has many brutal methods of teaching you that overspending is bad. If you get a raise, you decide where to spend the money.

Making a living off your art requires completely abandoning the employee mindset and *deciding* how you're going to live. This takes a business plan. While you can find great big books on developing a business plan, most of those are aimed at folks who want to run more traditional businesses and franchises. We're focusing on business planning for creators. The only tools required are your Bucket, a new spreadsheet, and your family's bills.

I cannot overemphasize that there is zero shame in deciding you don't want turn your art into your living. Relying on your art to feed the kids is not for everyone. You entirely own the choice and the responsibility. Once you accept both, any choice you make is correct for you.

There's also nothing wrong with trying the full-time creator thing, succeeding, and then deciding it isn't for you. It happens, and it's not unique to creative businesses. My wife's favorite bead store shut after three wildly successful years. The owner realized that what she really wanted was to play with sparkly beads all day, not manage the Bucket. You can stop at any time. Just try to exit gracefully, without trashing your finances.

If you keep waffling back and forth between trying full time and not, this chapter and the next might help you make up your mind. Think about your choices and options. Consider what you would gain, and what you would lose, and what you could change.

The Long Slow Slog taught you how to play Fill The Bucket. You've probably emptied the Bucket more than once—sometimes on purpose, sometimes accidentally. Creating full-time to pay the rent is like jumping from blackjack to no-limit poker. If you go bust, there is no day job to reseed your business. You're on your own.

But the rewards are *astonishing*.

First, start treating your life as a business.

This chapter starts with the absolute worst-case, most pessimistic assumptions, and improves from there.

The Bucket and Your Life

You have a Business Bucket. Money enters the Bucket irregularly. Some months it gets a drop or two. Other months, money pours in. You can't control how fast money enters the Bucket. The Long Slow Slog gives you context and experience for how your trade generates money, though. And we all hope that our next creation will be the thing that goes viral and makes a fortune.

We can't predict how much any one creation will make. If you use tools like Kickstarter you can get an idea, sure, but sometimes your best creation flops on its face and the most daft trivial thing you've done explodes. I might spend six months sweating over a book that sells only a hundred copies. I've spent a day slamming out a story I thought was one hundred percent unadulterated capybara dung, only to have it rocket off the shelves.[12] I have no way to predict anything.

The Bucket shows you how everything averages out, however. Experience has shown me that four books in a year lets me at least scrape by.

Earlier I said that the Bucket is a business machine that converts those irregular bursts of cash into a smooth, steady stream. My life is a hole in the bottom of the Bucket. The bigger the hole, the faster the Bucket drains. Rent and food and expenses are predictable, and subject to my control. Before I can control them, though, I must know what those expenses *are*.

Exploring Expenses

You have a handle on the expenses for your art. Now consider the expenses for your life.

If you want to make a living with your art, one of the important questions is "how much money do you need?" Set aside a couple hours and go through a calendar year of household expenses.

Make four lists, in a spreadsheet. Note how much you spend on each.

---

12   My editor assures me that while my assessment was correct, I underestimated the market for capybara dung.

- Stuff that your household pays for, but the business needs

- Stuff that your household pays for, but the business wants

- Stuff your household must have to function

- Stuff your household wants

We'll consider the first two lists, then the second two.

Business Expenses Paid By The Household

Consider the list of business-related expenses that your household pays for. Why is the business not paying for them? Most often, the answer is that you hadn't considered these expenses that way, yet.

Now that you have some experience watching the Bucket, take your lists to your accountant and have a chat. Which expenses can the business legally assume? If your art is making enough money that you're seriously considering the possibility of creating full time, shift those expenses over to the business. If you're not yet ready to make the jump, record them as you would any other expense the business can't yet take on.

If you're in the US and haven't read Nolo Press' *Tax Savvy for Small Business* yet, this is a great time to grab and devour a copy.

Household Needs and Wants

Firefighters say that everyone in a family must know where to meet in case of fire and that vital papers must be secured where they won't burn up. This is easy to set up beforehand, but really hard to agree on when the word *conflagration* is immediately applicable to your home.

In the same way, discussing financial disasters is easiest when you aren't under financial pressure. If you get laid off, you'll come home with a spinning head, churning emotions, and a pounding heart. You could find a worse time to make financial decisions, but it would probably involve black market organ transplants and an armored car heist.

If your income drops, what expenses will your household cut? What must you keep? The time to decide this is when everyone's employed, not under pink slip pressure. This discussion doesn't need to involve everyone; there's no need to worry the kids. (Once they're teenagers, having them listen to the discussion might be a useful education.) All decision makers must be included, though, and that'll vary depending on who's in your household.

Only you and your family knows what you need and want. I don't have cable TV, but if you have children the Disney Channel or Disney+ might be a legitimate need. My martial arts tuition might seem a pointless luxury to you, but my friends agree that some days, Lucas stomping off to punch something until he feels better is the only thing that keeps him out of jail. Brutally honest self-reflection is essential. What did you need to spend? What was excessive?

What can you scrape by with? What is utterly vital? What could go?

Perhaps the most difficult category is identifying things you did not strictly need, but you know dang well you're going to buy anyway even if it's not in the budget. Young Lucas' most frequent budget ruptures came from purchasing books, even when there was no money for them. My budgeting vastly improved once I looked in the mirror and conceded that I was an idiot who was going to buy books before food, and set aside money for it.

Make your choices. You can and will change them later. Perfection is not necessary. A starting list is. Preferably, a starting list with pessimistic-but-not-apocalyptic assumptions. Maybe all of my favorite authors will release a book in the same month, increasing expenses, but if I catch rose mosaic virus everything implodes anyway.

This is a family project. It's okay to make the first rough cut on your own, but discuss your lists with everyone involved in the business of your family. In case of financial disaster, maybe the kids would prefer to keep Netflix over Disney+. Perhaps firing the housekeeper and assuming personal responsibility for cleaning the toilets will lead to your spouse immediately divorcing you, but she's willing to take over mowing the lawn instead. Everybody has their own needs. Respect them.

Again, this is a *much* easier discussion when everybody has a job. Even if you don't become a full-time artist, having a list of stuff everyone agrees can be cut in case of financial disaster will save you so much stress when things go bad. At some point in your life, things *will* go bad.

The Business of Family

This exercise is exactly as complicated as your family's business. Yes, your household is another Bucket. Lots of households include two employed adults. It's common for husband and wife to both work, or for more complicated families to have multiple employed adults, or for one person to pay for the household. Retirees have pensions or Social Security or other savings. Multiple income streams are precious in any kind of business, including a family.

How you build your lists depends on how your family's business is arranged. If you're responsible for particular bills, include those bills on your list. If other folks have predictable incomes, include them. If other people's incomes are unpredictable, make your best guess. You've evolved a method to cope with your family's finances; leverage it.

For simplicity, my examples assume that one person supports the household.

Business Needs and Wants

Now that you've checked your household expenses for stray business expenses, revisit your business expenses. Once your Bucket has been running for a while, you'll understand your art's true cost.

Make separate lists of needs and wants, including the monthly cost for each item. Separating a creative business's needs from its wants is easier than a family's. For each expense, ask yourself two questions.

- Would not spending this money prevent you from practicing your art?
- Would your trade (the business of your art) stop without this expense?

If the answer to these questions is no, the expense is a want.

Just as for the family, make separate lists of the expenses for your business's needs and wants.

You *must* pay taxes and your accountant. Even countries that have modernized personal taxes down to one postcard per citizen have business taxes. Not paying your accountant is a great way to get in trouble with the tax agency. These are always business expenses.

You might also have expenses only applicable to your nation. In the United States, you must pay for healthcare and retirement. We'll discuss those later this chapter.

Some expenses arrive once a year: tax preparation, well-organized blackmail, eyeglasses, and so on. One of the big rules for running a small business is to never spend money you don't have. *Never.* It's much easier to save money to pay these throughout the year than scrape up the cash at the last minute. Divide all annual expenses by 12 and declare each to be monthly. No, you don't *pay* these bills monthly, but you *save* for them monthly. Make paying them as trivial as possible, and earn any interest as the money sits in your bank.

Your Financial Life: The Spreadsheets

Take your newly reassessed business and household expenses and put them in a single spreadsheet, with the monthly cost. If you're a spreadsheet maven you can put your family and your business on separate tabs, or use colors, or deploy other arcane tricks of spreadsheetery.

You'll end up with something like this, although your items and prices will be completely different than what I've chosen here.[13]

Family Essentials	Cost	Family Extras	Cost	Business Essentials	Cost	Business Niceties	Cost
Rent	$800	Lawn	$100	Internet	$100	Ads	$100
Food	$400	Cleaner	$200	Taxes	$300	Flunky	$200
...	...	...	...	...	...	...	...
Totals	$2000		$1000		$500		$500

You have four categories of expenses: business and personal, and essentials versus extras. Each category has a total, like so.

	Family	Business
Essential Spending Totals	$2000	$500
Extras	$1000	$500
Full Spending Totals	$3000	$1000

For ease of discussion, I'm going to call the minimum expenses Essential Spending. Your Essential Family Spending is what you need to keep your household basically functional. Essential Business Spending is the cost for you to keep your business going. When you add in the extras for each category, you get Full Family Spending and Full Business Spending.

---

13   My numbers are chosen to make the math of my examples easy to understand. Your numbers won't be.

The example household's Essential Family Spending is $2000 a month, but they routinely spend $3000 a month for Full Family Spending. Does that more or less match what really goes in and out of the family's bank account? If not, the example family missed something. They need to review their expenses and adjust their spreadsheets.

The business's Essential Spending is $500 a month, but they spend $1000 at Full Business Spending. Again, they need to verify that against their checkbook.

In total, this home and business spend $4,000 a month. In a financial emergency, they could cut this down to $2500 a month. Multiply everything by twelve to get $30,000 a year in annual Essential Expenses, and $48,000 in Full Expenses.

The first time through this exercise is grueling. I would not have made you do this if it wasn't so utterly essential to making a living as a creative. I'm not that much of a jerk.[14] Each time gets easier.

Expenses and The Bucket

Consider these expenses relative to the Bucket.

In our hypothetical example, your business Bucket, supporting only the business, has a $1000/month hole in the bottom. Money irregularly enters the Bucket, but you consistently take a thousand dollars out of it every month.

If you start paying your personal expenses out of the Bucket, you're expanding that hole to $4,000 dollars a month. If you subsist on Essential Expenses, you reduce that hole to only $2,500.

All through the Long Slow Slog, you've been watching the money level in the Bucket fill and empty. Have you earned over $30,000 a year consistently for a few years? In this hypothetical

---

14   Yes, yes, I know, I am kind of a jerk. I'm saying I'm not *that* much of a jerk. I have limits.

case, you could ditch the day job if you're willing to live with only Essential Spending. If you've consistently cleared $48,000 a year, you could maintain your current lifestyle.

If you make under $30,000 a year, your business does not make enough to support you. Depending on your craft, you might be able to increase your income by working more hours. It's best to know this before you start, as we'll discuss in "Planning for Failure" later this chapter.

Before flinging yourself into independence, consider what winning and losing at Fill The Bucket means for a full-time creator.

Winning and Losing

Winning at Fill The Bucket isn't traditional Western "winning." There is no end game, no victory lap, no trophy. Don't try to define "winning" as increased income; remember, you don't control how much money comes into the Bucket.

When you're making a living as an artist, winning is defined as "being able to live the life you want, doing the thing you love to do." Losing is anything less than winning.

The nice thing about losing as an artist is that you can always go back to the day job and create in your off hours. You've done it before. You know how this works. You can leverage your experience to build up resources and try again.

Most failures are due to undercapitalization.

Undercapitalization

You've probably heard the word *undercapitalized* flung about in news stories. It's a fancy way to say *a business doesn't have enough cash on hand to cover temporary problems*. Undercapitalization leads to failure. You must have enough money to get through hard times.

What do I mean, "hard times?" I'm writing this at the beginning of the pandemic of 2020. In the last five days restaurants, bars, libraries, and schools have all closed. There's widespread belief that the countermeasures are inadequate or excessive, depending on who you talk to. Nobody knows if we'll get through this fine or if millions of people will die. What we in the United States do know is that the stock market has plunged, many people have lost their jobs, and our nation's President has transformed a crisis into a debacle.

And everybody in the entire world has clamped down on unnecessary spending.

This is what business folks call a *black swan event.*

I'm a writer. Book sales have dropped eighty percent this week. The world's biggest single book retailer, Amazon, has announced that they're cutting shipping of non-essential goods. Depending on how bad this gets, books are not essential. Print books are half of my income.

Today, I am assuming that my little publishing empire will receive no income for six months, and that when money starts to appear again it will be very, very slow. How long can my business endure?

Suppose I had thirty thousand dollars in the bank. My essential spending is $2,500 a month. My funds would last for (30,000 ÷ 2500 =) twelve months. If I maintain full spending, at $4,000 a month, my funds would last for (30,000 ÷ 4000 =) seven and one half months.

Wow. That extra fifteen hundred dollars a month sucked away almost a third of my career. This illustrates one of the most important principles of cash flow: *fixed expenses harm your business.* We discuss this at length in Chapter 8.

Not everybody considers their risks this way. I expect to watch many businesses fail during this pandemic. Surely the big companies are prepared, though, right? You would think so, but a bunch of global airlines are already begging for bailouts.

They have had ten fantastic years of record profits, and spent those profits on stock buy-backs rather than saving for their future. They've run their businesses on quarter-to-quarter thinking.

You love creating. Making a living as a creator might well be your life's dream. I've known I wanted to be a writer since I discovered books were written by people and not handed down from a burning bush. Go find a mirror. Look at yourself firmly, set your jaw, narrow your eyes, and tell yourself, "Your art is more important, more precious to the world, than any stupid global airline." Plan accordingly.

My family is on Essential Expenses across the board. Because my ability to write my books is more important, more precious to the world, than any stupid global airline.

Not all disasters are global. Thinking that you are healthy and won't have any problems is a path to disaster. You are, at best, temporarily able-bodied.

I'd say I'm a basically healthy guy. Lying down on the floor and getting back up again is one of the hardest possible exercises, and I can do hundreds of falls in an hour on a tatami mat. A few years ago, I had appendicitis that turned to gangrene. This let me make a whole bunch of "rotten at the core" gags, but I couldn't write for two months. More recently, I had a thyroid cyst so big that if I turned my head to the right I blacked out. Another two months completely gone, plus reduced productivity for months beforehand when we didn't understand that something was squeezing my carotid artery and my already feeble little brain was literally starving.

My family had discussed our spending plans. Both my wife and I know what can be cut and when. Each time I crashed, She Who Must Be Obeyed immediately slashed the household back to Essential Spending. Also fortunately, each time I recovered fairly quickly. If I'd developed leukemia? Not so much.

I wish everyone a long and happy life with whatever sort of romantic partner(s) and extended family they have. From a planning perspective, every successful marriage ends in death and unsuccessful ones end in divorce. Either can spark or crush creativity. At best, you will wobble when either happens.

You can borrow money, sure. But it's either too early to borrow, or too late. Borrow early and you don't have a good enough track record to get a good rate. Borrow when your business is in trouble, and your business won't be stable enough to get a good rate. The time to borrow money is when you don't need it. And repayment is definitely an Essential Expense. Put the numbers in your spreadsheet and see what they do to your Bucket.

You are human. You *will* have health problems. You *will* suffer crippling heartache. These things are both inevitable and cannot be scheduled in advance. You will have unexpected times that you literally cannot work. Save money. Be sufficiently capitalized.

What is "sufficient capitalization?" I'm thrilled you asked. Sufficient capitalization lets you either stay in business, tighten the belt, or control failure. I express these with colors.

Red, Yellow, and Green

Financial distress, just like thyroid tumors and gangrene, destroys creativity. Creation comes out of the subconscious, and if your subconscious is fully occupied shrieking about the rent, it has no space left for your craft.

Exactly as deciding how to cut expenses the day you've been laid off is terrible, deciding on the strategy of your creative business when you're running in circles deciding between food and rent is terrible. Both problems have the same solution: make decisions beforehand, when you are relaxed.

Every decision you make involves some sort of measurement. Even something as vague as "I've eaten too much, I'm gonna pass on the third piece of pie" measures just how bloated your stomach is. "We don't have the money for that" measures your bank account. Before agreeing to go on a date you measure how creepy the other person seems, and probably bring your pepper spray anyway.

One of the reasons I call business a Bucket is because you can measure how much is in it. You can draw lines on the side to set levels. I cut the Bucket into three sections: Red, Yellow, and Green.

The Green section is at the top of the Bucket. When the money level is up in Green, life is good. You can live on Full Expenses, both personal and business. You have no cause to worry.

The Yellow section is in the middle of the Bucket. When the money level drops from Green into Yellow, you've crossed the Yellow threshold. You have reason for mild concern. Reduce your expenses to Essential Spending to get through this rough patch. It's possible to get into a situation where the Bucket sloshes back and forth across the Yellow threshold every month. If that happens, stay at Essential Expenses for a few months to build up a cushion.

When the money level drops below Yellow, you've crossed the Red threshold. Your business cannot sustain you. It's time to get back in the straight workforce.

Front-loading decisions relieves huge amounts of stress. Nightmares of going bust have awakened me at stupid o'clock more than once. Without these levels, I would worry for the rest of the night and be a completely unproductive wreck the next day. If I've set Yellow and Red thresholds, I can remind myself that the Bucket is at three times the Yellow threshold, way *way* up in the Green, and go back to sleep. Or that we're in

Yellow, but I have six months of expenses left and three books are coming out in those months.

How do you define levels? By time.

When I first calculated my Red and Yellow thresholds, the numbers startled me. These are worst case situations, to be used for measuring and guidance. We'll discuss both changing those numbers and reaching those lofty goals later this chapter. You'll also reassess these regularly.

Now all that remains is to set levels. Start with your failure plan.

The Failure Plan

No, you don't start by planning to fail. You start by saying "If I'm dependent on my business, and my business fails, what resources will I need to reenter the workforce without wrecking my family and my life?" The cliché that the best time to look for a job is when you have a job is not always true, but I guarantee that the worst time to look for a job is when you're flat broke. The answer here depends entirely on your skills and requires a hard look in the mirror.

Calculating your Red level, when it's time to give up on your own business supporting you, is all about how long it takes for you to find employment. My example calculations assume the worst case: I'm the sole breadwinner for my family, and that I'm bringing in zero money. You need Essential Spending in hand for each month you'll need to find a job.

Essential Spending x Months = Red Threshold

Additional breadwinners change your Essential Spending, but not the formula.

When your Bucket is low, you're already living on Essential Spending. Using the numbers from our last example, that's two thousand five hundred dollars a month.

So, what kind of cases might you have?

Let's start with the best possible failure plan: mine. I am stupidly lucky. The stuff I write includes nonfiction books on Internet engineering, and I am recognized as an expert on these topics. If I was to announce on any social media platform that I was on the market, offers would flood my inbox. While I could negotiate a comfortable position in a week, I want two months to find the best fit. My Red level equals two months of Essential Spending. Two months of expenses at two thousand five hundred dollars each equals a Red level of $5,000.

$$2 \times \$2,500 = \$5,000$$

If my Bucket ever drops below five thousand dollars, I'm done.

The other extreme? Public school teachers. Hiring takes place once a year. Many school systems have a rank-based system, where you start off as a part-time on-call substitute teacher and eventually accumulate enough seniority you can claim the least desirable position in the district. The most risk-tolerant teacher I interviewed said he would need two years of Essential Spending on hand before starting to look for a job. If his Essential Spending is also two thousand five hundred a month, and he needs twenty four months on hand, that's a Red level of $60,000.

$$24 \times \$2,500 = \$60,000$$

Ouch.

One teacher said she needed five years in the bank to consider creating full time. I don't have the heart to calculate that.

Remember, these are worst case analyses. We'll look at better cases.

The Failure Plan and Your Family

Your spouse won't take it well if you come home from the straight job one day and unexpectedly chortle that you turned in your two-week notice. Being part of a family might not mean communicating and supporting each other, but remaining in one does. An inability to discuss finances is a leading element of divorce. Unless you're responsible for and to yourself alone, involve your family in your failure plan.

Family support brings a whole bunch of advantages. If you're only responsible for half the bills, your Essential Spending is half what it could be. It also brings responsibilities and the need for compromise. I know that I could have a new job in a week, but She Who Must Be Obeyed is much more comfortable if I set a two-month Red level. Peace with my family is more important than a few thousand dollars resting in the Bucket—and if my Bucket drops that low, I'm in trouble anyway. Being conservative with your family's finances and safety is almost always the right decision.

Also discuss with your family what expenses and responsibilities could be shifted. This might not help with cash flow, but it definitely helps with getting family support. When I first became a full-time creator, I assumed the responsibility for taking an hour each morning and cleaning part of the house. Twice a week, even today, I take a five-minute break every ninety minutes and swap loads of laundry around.[15] As I stay home all day most days they're reasonable chores for me, bought my spouse's support, and frees up our precious weekends.

----

15 Yes, I know that some men won't even consider scrubbing the toilet and running the laundry as part of their household duties. If *this* is their show-stopper, they don't really want to create for a living.

Perhaps your contribution to the family bills is flexible. Maybe not. But it's worth discussing.

Family support can make your levels flexible. At one point, my company was brushing the Red threshold. I expected payments big enough to kick me well into Green within thirty days, but we were going to spend a couple weeks in the Red. I discussed the situation with She Who Must Be Obeyed. She agreed that the vendors who owed me money had paid their invoices on time for fifteen years, and that the company could handle a couple weeks in Red.

Yes, I discuss the Bucket with my family. Money is our society's last big taboo, but the successful creators I know all discuss money with their families. If you trust your family with your children and the capybara and to sign for you to have emergency surgery when you're unconscious because you caught the gangrene, you can discuss business with them too. Your family will call you on your daft decisions, point out perfectly obvious things you never considered, and in general help keep you from driving into the ditch.

Most countries consider a monthly company board meeting a reasonable expense, although the requirements vary. Our monthly board meetings are held at a restaurant. If we're in the Yellow, it's at the inexpensive Mexican place. Green demands sushi.[16] We discuss what happened this month and what's coming next. If you can't discuss money with your family, a few sessions with the right counselor helps immensely—and most probably will save your family as well as your business.

You'll especially want to involve them in setting your Yellow threshold.

---

16   If we're in a pandemic, it's fried chicken in the back yard— but *really good* fried chicken. Make Ragnarök as tax-deductible as possible.

The Yellow Threshold

Where Red is about recovering from failure, the Yellow threshold is about lifestyle. How long are you willing to endure living at Essential Expenses to have the job you want? No extras. No vacation. No cable TV, no meals out, no nothing. Bupkis. You are deliberately deciding to scrape by for this length of time. This is where you say "I'm gonna give it a year and see what happens." Again, this is a worst case analysis.

I know some creators whose answer is *forever*. I don't know that it's truly forever, but it's been multiple decades and despite occasional justified grousing about their own pigheadedness, they show no sign of quitting.

If you have family, the answer gets more complicated. Your family wants you to keep doing your art, because it makes you happy. But how many months are *they* willing to live at Essential Expenses level so that *you* can have the job you want? That's the core question. Maybe you're willing to go forever, but your spouse says a year. Or five years. Or never; it's full expenses or nothing. Get this all out before you set a number of months.

If you can't reach agreement, you're stuck with the time demanded by the person with the shortest tolerance. To do otherwise declares your business is more important than your loved ones. Remember back in Chapter 4 how it wasn't enough to say that your family came first, but you needed to *demonstrate* that at times? This is one of those times. A glad-hearted demonstration that you respect your family's needs and boundaries can often earn you some flexibility. Check in regularly, to see how risk tolerances have shifted.

Once you have a number of months, you can calculate the Bucket's Yellow threshold. Multiple the number of months you're willing to scrape by at Essential Spending by your monthly Essential spending, then add your Red threshold.

(Essential Spending x Months) + Red Threshold = Yellow Threshold

For example, my teacher friend and I both have absurdly supportive spouses willing to endure a year at Essential Spending ($2500 a month) before we get straight jobs. My Red threshold is five thousand dollars, so my Yellow threshold is $35,000. If I have more than $35,000 in the bank, I'm in the Green.

($2,500 x 12) + $5,000 = $35,000

My schoolteacher friend's Red threshold is $60,000, so his Yellow threshold is $90,000. He needs to have over $90,000 in the bank, almost three times my level, to be in the Green.

($2,500 x 12) + $60,000 = $90,000

Ouch again.

The Red and Yellow thresholds are measurement tools. The next chapter discusses what to measure, and how.

"Measurements and the Worst Case Scenarios" Action Items

1. Create an empty spreadsheet like that shown in *Your Financial Life: The Spreadsheets*.

2. Examine what your household has spent in the last year. If you are responsible for the entire household, consider the entire household. If you contribute only for certain bills, look at those bills. Get your checkbook, credit card statements, and other bills. Put them in a spreadsheet, as discussed in *Exploring Expenses*. How much do you spend in your personal life? Does that roughly equal your income? If you pay cash for your bills, estimate. You can always refine later.

3.   Should any of those expenses be business expenses? If so, see if you can move them to your business, as per *Business Expenses Paid By The Household*.

4.   Involve your family's decision makers, and consider needs and wants. Make a spreadsheet of each, listing totals. Imagine each breadwinner lost their job. Discuss what you'd cut, and what you'd have to do for each job loss. Break what you pay into two lists, Household Essential Spending and Household Extra Spending. I talk about all this in *Household Needs and Wants*. Reassure each other that you'd all like this discussion to remain purely theoretical and distribute affection as needed.

5.   Revisit your business expenses. Reassess your needs and wants, as discussed in *Business Needs and Wants*.

6.   Consider your savings, as discussed in *Undercapitalization*. What is your household's total Essential Spending? How long could you subsist on that? Is it time to trim back to Essential Spending and stash some cash?

7.   Imagine you went full time and it didn't work out, as we discuss in *The Failure Plan*. How long would it take you to get your old job back? Calculate what you think your bucket's Red Threshold is. Put it in your Expenses Spreadsheet, so that when you change the number of months the Red Threshold automatically updates.

8.   Imagine you've gone full time, it went well for a while, and then you develop a serious illness, like I talk about in *The Yellow Threshold*. How many months should your business realistically be able to endure with you making zero income? Use this to calculate what you think your Yellow Threshold is.

9. Once your family has recovered from the last discussion, discuss your failure plan with them just like in *The Failure Plan and Your Family*. Work together to agree on numbers that make everyone comfortable. Use the spreadsheets to make calculations easy.

10. Develop the habit of revisiting and reassessing your business expenses monthly. Put it on your calendar.

11. Work with your family towards revisiting household expenses monthly.

Chapter 7: Jump or Be Pushed?

In an ideal world, you would save enough money to put yourself solidly in Green before jumping to full-time creative self-employment.

This would be nice. This…does not happen.

Creators who go full-time either change the game or ride a crisis.[17] They jump, or they're pushed.

Change the Game

You can't control how much money comes in, but you *can* dictate how much money comes out. What are you willing to do to have the life you wish? What sorts of risks can you tolerate?

I know one writer (JC Andrijeski) who found that her income would let her live very comfortably—in Thailand. She moved to Bangkok with a couple suitcases, wrote her fingers off, and eventually made enough that she could move back to Los Angeles. She's hard-core, but JC was responsible for only herself. If she failed, she was the only person who would wind up begging for scraps on a street corner while fending off hungry capybaras and hoping tonight's dysentery wouldn't be too awful. Those of us with families must be more risk-averse.

Look at your life. Where do you live? Can you move some place cheaper? While New York City has a history as a creative and cultural center, the truth is very few full-time creators live there anymore. It's far too expensive. I've visited California more than once. Not only are homes expensive; so are groceries, gasoline, water, and probably oxygen.

---

17   A very few full time creators are initially supported by their spouse. That's great if you can arrange it, but it's not an actionable strategy.

A key part of my business is that I live in Michigan. If I lived anywhere except cuddled up to Detroit, my mortgage payments would be three times bigger. A few years ago, the city was selling foreclosed homes for $500. My wife and I seriously considered moving, but we'd just finished repainting our current home and I was still in the *I am never touching a paint brush again* phase.

If you'll need years to get a new job in your current career, but you want to be a full-time creator, maybe your failure plan should include starting in a different career. Scrutinize your world. Where is there a need? In 2020 in the United States, the market is desperate for electricians, plumbers, and welders. Not only do you start with wages well above the national average, you get paid for the two years you're in school. This would substantially reduce your Red threshold.

Becoming a full-time creative upends your life. If it fails, well, your life is already upended. You might as well land in a secure, tolerable place.

Study your Essential Expenses and your Extra Expenses. If you were to make massive structural changes in your life, how low could you drag them?

Riding the Crisis

Many full-time creatives go full time when life smacks them. Layoffs, failed employers, and life disasters put them in crisis, and their trade let them resolve the crisis. The Red and Yellow thresholds, combined with your Essential and Full Expenses, are tools to help you decide if you can or cannot use your trade to resolve your crisis. If you've already discussed the underlying financial issues with your family, you have a common basis for discussion. By nurturing the Bucket all throughout the Long Slow Slog, you've demonstrated to everyone (including yourself) that your craft is adequate, your art is good enough, and that your trade works.

Using your trade to resolve the crisis involves a whole bunch of negotiation and trading. In a crisis, all those theoretical discussions from the last chapter are suddenly very real. You go to cut the extra expenses, and it turns out that some of them are not so extra. This is where you agree to take over certain chores in exchange for your spouse's support, and work assiduously to earn enough that you can hire someone to clean up after you.

Income and the Bucket

We haven't discussed income much, because you don't control it. While working hard, improving your craft, practicing your art, and learning your trade all enhance your chances of making money, other people's purchasing decisions are beyond your control. What matters is how much the Bucket's level rises over a year, or two years, or even five years.

If you made over a year's worth of Essential Expenses last year, maybe you could make a go of it. If you made over five years' worth of Full Expenses over the last five years, you could almost certainly make a go of it.

My Essential Expenses for both home and business total $2,500 a month. That's $30,000 a year. Did I add more than $30,000 to the Bucket last year? If so, and if spending the additional time at my art and my craft has a reasonable chance of increasing my income, I have a decent chance.

If I added less than $30,000 to the Bucket, it's a lot more iffy. How confident are you that working like an obsessed artist will boost your income?

Experience in your trade offers great hints of what's possible and what isn't. While there are zero guarantees that your trade will support you, there are also zero guarantees that your next straight job won't be awful.

Making the Decision

Your life hits a crisis. Should you jump into full time as a creative? If your business' yearly income exceeds your Essential Expenses, or even your Full Expenses, and your Bucket is way up in Green, do it.

Again, this never happens. In the real world, we have to act on experience, logic, and hope for just a touch of luck. Everybody's decision is unique.

In my case, I had chosen a technology job that gave me a lower salary in exchange for being treated like an actual person and a total[18] absence of company stupidity. Five years later, the company went under. If I returned to a standard corporate gig, my salary would double. So would my stress and my weight. Family dinners would vanish, just like the bad old days. Over on the artistic side, though, I was making nearly as much from my art as from the day job. The Bucket was in the lower end of Yellow and making more than Essential Expenses.

I discussed the situation with She Who Must Be Obeyed. We agreed that I should jump to writing full time. We would go on Essential Expenses for a year and see what happened.

For the next year, I wrote like an obsessed maniac scribbling on his padded walls. A standard corporate job demands nine- and ten-hour days from their technology staff. I treated my craft and my trade like such a job and refused to spend a penny that wasn't absolutely necessary. I wrote seven books that year and published six of them. At the end of the year, I broke into Green.

Sometimes you get pushed into full-time creation, but your Bucket doesn't get enough income yet. Treat your creative business as a part-time job, and look for other ways to bring

---

18   Okay, fine, "nearly total." Nobody's perfect, not even that boss.

in income, such as teaching or tutoring. Such gigs have the advantage of getting your name more widely known in your trade. I know more than one artist who edits, coaches, and speaks about their art to augment their income.

Suppose one of my school-teacher friends gets laid off from his job. He's going to need two or more years to secure a new position. He must change school districts, which means selling his house. His trade brings in money, but his Bucket doesn't quite fill up quickly enough to meet his expenses. Why not move to some place with a really cheap cost of living, where they're desperate for teachers? Pick up the odd substitute teaching gig when he can get it, and art super hard when there's no work? Maybe he can assemble a living wage out of multiple jobs, and increase how much he makes as an artist.

If you can't drain Essential Expenses from the Bucket every month without slipping into the Red, your trade is not yet viable. It is not yet the time to jump to full-time creation. Knowing your personal Red and Yellow Thresholds, and documenting your Essential and Full Expenses, lets you easily make those decisions.

Your Life in Colors

The Red, Yellow, and Green parts of the Bucket offer guidance on the health of your trade. A long-term creative uses them to guide not only their business, but their life.

Living in the Red

Many non-creatives live their entire lives in the Red. Debts, often involuntarily or ignorantly assumed, chain people to a paycheck-to-paycheck life. A changing economy abandons innumerable hard-working people. Automation obsoletes entire professions. Here in the United States, innocently paying a deceased parent's last electric bill from your checkbook can leave your family legally responsible for all their debts. An unexpectedly deceased or divorced spouse can lead to ruin. Many countries have chosen economic systems that either deliberately or inadvertently impose unreasonable burdens on the lower classes.

Here's an ugly secret: many corporations, from big global firms to tiny ones you've never heard of, also exist in the Red. They are machines for processing money, and they have chosen to expand their operations so that they have just enough coming in today to pay yesterday's bills. When these companies do well, they pay the executives lavish bonuses and buy back their own stock. When the economy craters, they can no longer meet their bills and immediately implode. Whenever the United States economy crashes, all of the airlines based here start begging for handouts. Huge chunks of the economy are based on scraping by.

If you gotta scrape by, you might as well scrape by with a creative trade. Maybe you can get a few tax deductions. Living in the Red takes guts and determination, no matter your career. It also takes far more financial help than I can offer you. All I can advise you is to think long-term as much as possible, but feed the kids today.

Living In The Yellow

In Yellow you're better off than those folks living Red, but not where you want to be. That's better than many people ever manage. Congratulate yourself.

Yellow is also the most dangerous zone for a new professional creator. If you have tens of thousands of dollars in the bank, why shouldn't you spend some of it? Isn't that what life is about? Surely you deserve to live a better life and boost your expenses!

You can choose to do this.

The question is, what is your goal?

The goal of a creative career is to spend your life doing things you love doing. Not this month of your life. Not this year. Your life. All of it. Maybe you'll switch to writing children's books or training stunt-parachuting capybara teams, but the plan is to remain free of outside employment *forever*. Money is both a tool to achieve that goal, and a consequence of living that life.

After a while, living at only Essential Expenses might wear on you. You might decide that you'd rather get a straight job than endure months living on only Essential Expenses. If so, you misjudged what was Essential and what was Extra.

It is okay to discover that Younger You was wrong. It's not only okay to change your assessments, it is *expected*. If you realize that spending the extra money each month for a specific luxury will keep you sane, put it on your spreadsheets and see how that alters your finances. If it means you'll need another month or two to hit Green, but you'll be happier during those months, go right ahead. The only requirement is that you be honest about your evolving needs, wants, and actions.

As long as you live in the Yellow and create full time, however, you have the opportunity to increase your income. Every creation is a chance to hit it big. I would be delighted to hit that jackpot. I hope that the book you're reading right now hits the jackpot. It's more realistic, however, to understand that with each thing you create, a few more people discover your work.

I deliberately practice my craft with every book I write, and push to express myself through my craft. Practicing a specific skill with each book means that each one is automatically "the same, but different." My art improves, my market expands. I'll have about forty books out before the end of this year, plus flocks of shorter pieces. Each title adds a brick to my fan base. A career built from forty bricks is inexorable, and makes winning the lottery unnecessary. A lottery win would delight me, mind you, but it's unnecessary.

As long as your income exceeds your expenses, your Bucket is filling up. You will reach Green.

Yellow is not there to restrict you, but to give you time to correct course before sinking into Red. Reassessing your expenses and thresholds is necessary. If you've been sitting pretty up in Green, don't panic when an unexpected problem plunges you into Yellow. If your income regularly exceeds expenses, you're doing okay.

Maybe you set yourself a three-month limit on Yellow, but you realize it'll take you six months to earn your way out of it. You can decide to accept that, or not. Maybe you realize that a couple of Extra expenses are really Essential if you're stuck in Yellow for years. That's also fine.

In the long game, though, you'll be happier if you can save enough to get yourself solidly into Green.

Living In The Green

If you're above the Yellow threshold, you're in the Green. You can pay yourself your full expenses. You have achieved your ideal life. Spend two minutes congratulating yourself and thanking your loved ones for their support, schedule one heck of a party for the weekend, and get back to work.

Achieving Green doesn't mean you can stop watching the Bucket. The Bucket is like a toddler who's just discovered the miraculous delight of energy drinks. Without supervision it'll spill its juice box on the dog, strip off its clothes, and run into traffic. Watch your expenses. Make sure the level in the Bucket constantly increases, or at least doesn't go down.

Oh, and throwing a monster party for those who support your business, and their families? Totally a business expense. Just don't make it fancy enough to knock you back down into Yellow.

No matter what level you spend your time in, you won't be able to play Fill The Bucket forever.

Endgame: Failure

Suppose you don't make it. You gave it your best shot, soared for a time, and life or the trade kicked you down into Red. Perhaps you listened to advice from some nutjob who spoke really confidently about yellow buckets with holes in them, made a plan, saved your resources, and leaped into full-time creative work the month before an economic crash shut down the economy.[19]

The good news is, you don't have to quit creating. You're back in the Long Slow Slog, creating in your free time like you did for years.

What should you do with your business when you go back to full-time employment? That's a highly individual decision. Despite what well-meaning friends and colleagues will tell you, *any choice you make is correct for you.* If you need to temporarily stop your trade to overcome heartbreak or overwork or rage, that's fine. If you convert your art to a pure hobby, that's also all right. If you shut down the time-consuming parts of your trade and focus on the joyful but profitable bits, that's ideal.

We creative sorts are stubborn. Some uncharitable sorts might even describe us as "pigheaded." Failing in your first business is very common. You can try again. Once you recover from the emotions of failing, consider how you failed. Maybe it's as simple as undercapitalization. Some artists go under because they don't understand their trade well enough. Others sign ill-considered contracts.

You've failed many times in your art. Why should your first run at business be any better? Using the Bucket and the Red, Yellow, and Green values will help you make better decisions, though.

---

19   Dear you-know-who-you-are: I'm *so* sorry. So, so sorry.

Endgame: Success

Suppose you are wildly successful. You get to live the life you want to live, for years or decades, until you get too old to work anymore. Remember, art as a living is a long game. In sufficiently long terms, you are only temporarily healthy. You must save for your dotage.

The good news is, retirement savings are tax deductible in most countries. Talk to your accountant. Save money for Older You.

Health Care in the USA

There is no use creating for a living in your youth only to end up an arthritic geezer living under an overpass gazing covetously at the folks strong enough to claim a refrigerator box—or, arguably worse, dead young because you couldn't afford your diabetes meds. People living in the United States must directly fund their own healthcare. If you are wildly successful at your trade and millions of dollars into the Green, you can pay cash for everything. Otherwise, buy health insurance.

The US system is designed for corporations and distinctly hostile to independents. I would have been a full-time writer in 2003 except for the utter impossibility of buying insurance that covered my family's pre-existing conditions. Once the Affordable Care Act passed, buying that insurance became possible if not inexpensive. That was a key point in my decision to jump.

The state-run health insurance exchanges are certainly an option. The plans offered there are not the same as what is offered to businesses, however. The differences between exchange and business plans vary by state, but health insurance brokers can help you sort out the differences. You don't pay brokers directly; their fees are paid by the insurance companies.

Suppose you discover that you need a business-level health plan?

Go back to the absolute basics. *A business is an artificial entity for processing money.* It isn't an employer. It isn't a way to pay your rent. Buying insurance is manner of processing money. Look for an opportunity to process money in a way that allows you to buy the health plan you need. If the opportunity doesn't exist, build it.

Perhaps the simplest option is to join the local Chamber of Commerce. Many creatives consider the CoC a den of staid businessmen, sleazy real estate developers, and assorted shysters. That might even be true. Many Chambers offer opportunities for members to buy into business-grade health care plans, however.

That's not viable? Find another small independent not in your immediate family who wants the same level of health care coverage you do. It doesn't matter if they're another creative or if they own a dry cleaning business. You might even find them at the local Chamber of Commerce meeting. Join with them to create a limited liability company with the purpose of "creative services" or "support for independent employers" or some generic thing like that. Have the LLC buy health care as a business. You'll pay a few bucks for an accountant to administer the LLC, but it's far cheaper than paying for a fully wired vacation in the intensive care unit.

Or, you could always move to a country with a civilized health care system. Like Thailand.

"Jump or be Pushed" Action Items

1. Get a piece of paper. Divide it into two columns, "Would Do" and "Wouldn't Do." Reread *Change the Game*, then sit on your own and think what you're willing to do to make a living as a creative. Would you be willing to move to Thailand? Would you do something truly terrifying, like move to Detroit? Perhaps most dire of all: would you move back in with your parents? Brainstorm all the options you can think of and write them down in one column or another. Sort out for yourself how far is too far.

2. Now that you know how far you are willing to go, sit down with your family's decision makers and ask them what they are willing to put up with. This is best done early in your career, when the discussion is purely theoretical. Their wishes will change over time, but you need a place to start.

3. In much of the world, "I'm making a living as an artist" is slang for "I'm sponging off my family." Tell your family that the goal of an artistic career is to build your craft, art, and trade into something that will help the family, and that you don't want them to support you.

4. Spend one hour researching online about funding retirement for independent business people in your country. Do not give your name, email, or phone number to any web site or any variety of broker; they will spend the rest of their days hounding you for business. One hour will suffice to learn the shape of your options.

5. If you are in the United States, find the web page for your local Chamber of Commerce. See if they offer health insurance. Even if your spouse's job provides health insurance, you should know if you have an easy alternative.

Chapter 8: Cash Flow Doom

For many creators, good news is bad news. "A million dollars just landed in the Business Bucket! Tesla leases all around!"

"I just signed a Hollywood shopping agreement for one of my novels! We're gonna be rich!"

"The economy has tanked, but we're doing well. Carry on for now."

The most insidious? "I can now afford to have someone else do the work I loathe."

These are all bad in that they encourage you to make the same wrong decision: increasing your fixed expenses. Fixed expenses harm a business.

A *fixed expense* is money that you must pay on a regular schedule. Rent is a fixed expense. You can move to a place with cheaper rent, but moving costs money and steals time from creation. Cable TV is a fixed expense. You can get rid of it, but cable companies demand you brave the Minotaur's Labyrinth to reach the cancellation desk. Your mortgage is a very fixed expense; getting rid of it will occupy you for *months*. Insurance is a fixed expense. Taxes aren't exactly fixed, but they sure recur.

It is okay to spend money, if you do it correctly.

How Not To Spend Money

Expected income is tantalizing. The check is going to arrive in thirty days, so maybe you can splurge today? That money is not real and cannot be spent until it has been resting in your bank account for a few days.

Why be so paranoid? Maybe you had a massive Amazon sales spike this month, but what if Amazon's inscrutable algorithm declares those sales fraudulent and they suspend your account rather than pay up? Contracts can be violated, invalidated, or contested. Suppliers and customers can go bankrupt. Customers can flat-out refuse to pay you. Maybe they'll refuse with a sneer, daring you to do anything about it. Maybe they'll blame it on the economy and regretfully return your gently-used art.

All of these happen. Things worse than these happen.

The proper splurge for a big sale that will be paid later is, say, an ice cream cone.[20] It is not a new car.

Different Types of Expenses

Not all spending is equal. You must differentiate between one-off expenses, investments in the business, and fixed expenses.

One-off expenses are things that you decide to splurge on. The million-dollar check arrives, and you decide to trade in your 1997 Corolla for an up-to-date electric? That's a one-off expense. You have the money. You're choosing to spend it. A party for your suppliers and supporters to celebrate your good fortune is a one-off expense. Inviting your enemies and detractors to the "I Rule You Drool Banquet" is also a one-off. One-off expenses are indulgences, and a business can decide to indulge. These one-off expenses scoop money from the Bucket once.

An *investment* is a one-off expense that will help your business. Upgraded tools? Classes and conferences? A consultation with an intellectual property attorney about licensing your figurines to a manufacturer? Anything that enhances your art, craft, or trade is an investment. Investments might or might not pay off, but you purchase them with the

---

20   Don't skimp. Get *good* ice cream.

intent that they will pay for themselves. Investments also scoop money from the Bucket, lowering its level, but it's a one-time drop.

Fixed expenses are monies that you must pay on a schedule. They increase the size of the hole in your Bucket, releasing money more quickly. They change your Red and Yellow Thresholds.

How Fixed Expenses Wreck Businesses

Remember the formulas for calculating Red and Yellow Thresholds.

Red Threshold = Essential Spending x Months

Yellow Threshold = (Essential Spending x Months) + Red Threshold

We'll use these to see how fixed expenses play out in reality.

The Stable Business

Your business has grown to the point where you have a separate studio, with its own electrical and heating bills. You've chosen to accept this expense rather than argue continuously with your spouse about filling the garage with the massive kiln and the ranks of undelivered clay pots.

After years of creative work, you've boosted your average income to a little over five thousand dollars a month. Experience tells you that you have a holiday surge in the autumn and a smaller dip in winter.

Your Full Spending is now $5,000 a month, but if the economy faceplants you can cut back to Essential Spending of $3,000. You also spend an hour or two a day cleaning up after yourself, and a couple more hours each day doing low-level tasks that could be performed by a half-trained capybara.

Let's assume you have excellent job prospects, and only need two months to find a job. Your Red threshold is $6,000.

$$\$3,000 \times 2 = \$6,000$$

If the economy crashes, people are not going to visit the boutiques where your pots are sold. You want your business to be able to endure twelve months of zero income. Your Yellow threshold, twelve months at $3,000 a month, is $42,000

$$(\$3,000 \times 12) + \$6,000 = \$42,000$$

You have fifty thousand dollars in the Bucket, so you're inarguably Green. The Bucket even gains a few thousand dollars a year.

Then you make a sale for fifty thousand dollars.

Destabilizing Yourself

The great big check arrives and—wonder of wonders—it doesn't bounce and the customer doesn't cancel it! At one hundred thousand dollars, the Bucket looks crazy full. It's time to spend some money and improve your trade.

It's obviously time to hire an employee. The flunky can clean up the place and perform other low-level chores. The flunky can even talk to customers, leaving you free to wholly commit your art!

You head down to FlunkyMart and discover that good flunkies are not cheap. If you're lucky you could get a cheap flunky who's responsible and energetic and willing, but if you're not they might be better suited for a career in one-fingered nasal excavation. Even if you find an enthusiastic cheap flunky, you're gonna spend a bunch of your time training the critter.

So you get a good flunky. One who's skilled and friendly and has a shiny coat and wags whenever he sees you.

Poof! Your Essential Spending *and* your Full Spending just jumped by $5,000 a month. That's not only the flunky's salary; that's employment taxes and rabies shots and all the other little things an employer must provide a flunky. Your

Essential Spending is $8,000 a month, while your Full Spending is $10,000 a month.

Let's check your thresholds.

Your Red threshold is $16,000.

$$(2 \times \$8,000) = \$16,000$$

Your Yellow threshold is a whopping $102,000.

$$(12 \times \$8,000) + \$16,000 = \$102,000$$

You have $100,000 in the bank. You just got a big check, doubling your money, and because of one single decision, you've dropped right back in Yellow. Not far into Yellow. You're so close to Green that you can lick it. Surely you can save your way into it, right?

Worse and Worse

You spend $3,000 a month on yourself, and $5,000 on your flunky. You're in this ridiculous position where your brand-new flunky has a better lifestyle than you do. But you're the boss! You own the company! *How did this happen*???

It happened because you didn't want to do parts of the work. You hired a flunky to answer the phone, lug boxes, and clean the studio.

But wait. It gets worse.

It's taken you years to build your trade to five thousand dollars a month. Your minimum expenses are eight thousand dollars a month. That great big check will carry you for a while, but if you keep losing three thousand dollars a month you will go out of business. Even if that flunky brings you an extra three thousand dollars a month of productivity, can you sell half again as many pieces?

Probably not.

No, that's not the worst.

All that work the flunky is going to do for you? Even if they have all the required skills, you have to teach them how *you* want it done. When you do the work yourself, it gets done in precise accordance with your art. Your art changes every day. You must spend a chunk of time every single day directing your flunky in how you want it done. If you're lucky enough to get a flunky who can read minds, you're not paying them near enough.

And your flunky has their own life. Things happen in people's lives. Your Yellow Threshold is calculated based on you getting sick, but what happens when your flunky blows his appendix or loses a parent? You're out their help. It'll happen at the worst possible time for you, because that's how life works. You're paying someone without getting the benefit of their presence.

It's not done getting worse.

Your flunky is not a thing. As people, employees are human beings and not disposable. Respect them as such. Their employment with you, though? That's totally disposable. Employees go on the Extra Expenses side of the spreadsheet. When times get hard, they have to go.

I know multiple writers and artists who hired friends to handle their scut work. When the Bucket sank through Yellow towards Red, they chose to let their business tank rather than face firing a friend. Placing your friendship ahead of your business is a valid decision, but consider ahead of time what that decision will be.

Firing a friend absolutely sucks. The reason you have to fire them might not even be your fault. Maybe the national or global economy imploded. In my lifetime, the United States economy has pulled a shiv every ten years or so. You will have to fire that friend right when times are most hard.

Or, still worse? That flunky's work is crap. Can you look at a friend and tell them that their work is inadequate and you're firing them?

The obvious answer is to find a flunky who isn't a friend. If they're a good flunky, though, you're going to like them. They might even become a friend. Firing them because of an economic downturn is gonna suck.

This is precisely why I have no employees. I do not have the personality to fire people with a clear conscience.

I strongly suspect that some bosses present themselves as jerks to protect themselves emotionally when they must let people go. It doesn't excuse their behavior, mind you, but it's certainly human.

Eliminating Fixed Expenses

Do you *need* the new studio, or merely *want* it? You could have your company lease a car for you, but how do you feel about that car being repo'd during the next debacle?

If you truly need something, try converting it to a one-time expense or an investment. You need a new car? Fine. Dip into the Bucket and buy it. Maybe it will knock you back down into Yellow, but what you're doing is borrowing money from yourself. Why give someone else interest payments? If the worst part of your day is two hours of cleaning up after yourself, maybe hire an outside service. That'll be cheaper than an employee and easier to get rid of.

If you're the recipient of fixed expenses, you call it *recurring revenue*. Companies love recurring revenue. Recurring revenue is not creative, but it comes every month. Their recurring revenue is your loss. Any time someone mentions recurring revenue or easy payments, consider which side of the equation you are on.

Every time you examine the Bucket, check your recurring expenses. Have you added any more? Have any of the existing ones grown? Hunt them out. Eradicate all that you can. Develop a finely trained and deeply ravenous Fixed Expense Hunter-Killer Instinct.

Increasing Fixed Expenses

I only increase Full or Essential expenses when both of two conditions apply.

First, I must have enough cash in hand to keep the business above the Yellow Threshold for an entire year at the increased level, assuming *zero* income for that year. While adding a fixed expense to my company is not a magic spell to crash the economy, it sure feels that way sometimes.

Second, after adding the new expense, my income must exceed the new Full Expenses. If I hire a flunky, I must be making enough money to fully pay both the flunky and myself. In the last example, when hiring a flunky raised my Full Expenses to $10,000 a month? I must consistently average over $10,000 a month in income before hiring the flunky.

Before increasing fixed expenses, consider how those increased expenses affect your long term dreams and goals. I have a dream of writing enough to pay off the mortgage. (It's a dream because I influence but don't directly control my income.) Hiring an employee or buying a new car works against that dream.[21]

If you want to do something that would increase your fixed expenses, consider other ways to accomplish that same task. Rather than employees, I've assembled a team of freelancers that provide different services, and I pay them both well and

---

21   The dream of paying off your thirty year mortgage with your art gets *much* easier if you wait twenty-nine years and eleven months. Everything is numbers.

promptly. Contractors know we're all in the same position, and during downturns many are willing to negotiate, swap services, or take payments over time. We all know making *something* beats being broke.

Before committing to spend any money on an ongoing basis, do your very best to come up with some way to weasel out of it. Only increase fixed expenses if you have absolutely no other choice.

Economic Crashes

Not all of your trade problems originate from your bad decisions. At any moment, at least one country in the world suffers from a lousy economy. One day, it will come to you. Unless you are extraordinarily lucky, these problems will affect you.

When economic disaster hits, you have a few options.

You could carry on as you have been, hoping that the troubled times pass before you go broke. You maintain full staff, use your contractors as frequently as ever, and continue the daily chilled sherbet delivery. If the disaster passes quickly, you're fine and everybody thinks you're a great person. If the troubles persist for too long, your business goes under and you join everybody else at the food bank and homeless shelter. I know more than one creative business that managed to stretch their funds through troubled times. More than one made it to the beginning of the recovery, but didn't have enough cash to pay everyone's salaries through the recovery. They imploded right when times were looking up.

You could immediately drop down to Essential Expenses, maximizing how long you can stay in business. You reduce outside contracting, lay off all but the most vital employees, whack fixed expenses, and brutally interrogate every penny before permitting it to leave your business. People might think you're paranoid.

Or, you can do something in between. How much do you spend on that daily sherbet delivery? Is a weekly hairdo for the office capybara truly necessary? Will cutting them extend your company's lifetime?

I'm not saying you have to do any particular one of these. I am saying you must choose one.

How do you choose? When the economy turns sour, make a copy of your expenses spreadsheet and play with things. How long will your cash on hand last if you fire everyone, ditch the studio, and move back into the garage? How about if you keep the people, but have everyone work from home? How do different changes affect your Yellow and Red Thresholds? Remember that you don't know how long the trouble will continue, and that money won't arrive in your bank account until a few months after the recovery. Everything boils down to *how long will your cash on hand last?*

My goal is to spend my entire life in creative work that I love doing. When disaster hits, I immediately slash expenses. Wearing my Business Hat, I'll even drop projects currently in production but not yet released if need be.

Human beings are a complicated tangle of rationality and rationalization, and we don't always understand which we act from. Any time you consider spending money, especially on a recurring basis, eliminate your impatience and do the math first. Consider how that expense changes how your Bucket fills when times are good, and when times go bad.

Decide ahead of time. Will you let your trade go bankrupt? Or will you hold your dream for the rest of your life?

"Cash Flow Doom" Action Items

1. The four most common things folks want out of a career in the arts are personal satisfaction, the freedom to create, to make an impact, and fame. Some of these desires might be minuscule—if I truly wanted fame, I would write different books. Think about what you want from your art and your life. If you want something different, add it to the list. Rank these things in order. Recognize that no matter which you most desire, every single one of them requires your trade to continue.

2. Ask your sweetest, tenderest friend to help you test something by pretending to be your employee for two minutes. They will—they're sweet. Imagine they're your employee and depending on you to feed their children. Look them in the eye and say, "Your work is not good enough. You're fired." Say it like you mean it. Can you do that? Even when their eyes get big and they start to blubber? Can you say "I know people are lined up at the food banks hoping a scrap of bread is left by the time they get to the front. You're fired anyway." Once you apologize profusely and everyone recovers from you breaking their heart, repeat the experiment with the friend voted Most Likely To Punch The Boss In The Face. Before you ever hire someone, remember what these experiences felt like.

3. Make a list of the tasks of your craft and your trade you might one day need help with. For each, write down what sort of person could provide that help without bringing them on as a full-time employee. You will be amazed what services you can get on a contract basis.

4. Look at your Essential and Extra Expenses. Which of these are fixed expenses? Get those bills. Look at the details of each. Are you paying for any extra services on any of them? How much do you pay for those services over one year? Do you need them? A key example is replacement service on a cell phone. $30 a month is $360 a year. You could purchase a new phone for that, on the off chance that you happen to lose it. Of course, if you lose your phone twice a year, then you're taking the cell phone company for a ride and I am compelled to approve.

Afterword

I hope that this little book has taught you how to think about business, cash flow, and money in a way that you find useful.

Business isn't magical. It's a skill, like dry cleaning or cooking decent hamburgers. Business is a necessary skill for a life of joyful creativity. If a chef can manage to run a business while cooking fifteen hours a day and keeping all her flunkies employed, you can do the same for yourself. If you remember nothing else from this book, absorb these three things.

Business is a long game.

So is a creative life.

And if you keep your eye on your Bucket, you can win at both.

Patronizers

That bit where I said you should list all of your possible income sources, and decide which to use? I use Patreon. Those fine folks at the "Career Supporter" level—Jeff Marracini, Kate Ebneter, Philip Vuchetich, and Stefan Johnson—get their names in the back of the print and electronic versions of every book I put out.

My sincere gratitude to every one of you, and to all those folks who support me in any way. You make my creative career a whole bunch easier.

About the Author

Full time author Michael W Lucas has written thirty-odd books so far, and experts doubt he can be stopped. Learn more at www.mwl.io.

Novels (as Michael Warren Lucas)

Immortal Clay
Kipuka Blues
Butterfly Stomp Waltz
Terrapin Sky Tango
Hydrogen Sleets
git commit murder

Nonfiction (as Michael W Lucas)

Absolute BSD — Absolute OpenBSD (1st and 2nd edition)
Cisco Routers for the Desperate (1st and 2nd edition)
PGP and GPG — Absolute FreeBSD (2nd and 3rd edition)
Network Flow Analysis — SSH Mastery (1st and 2nd edition)
DNSSEC Mastery — Sudo Mastery (1st and 2nd edition)
FreeBSD Mastery: Storage Essentials
Networking for Systems Administrators
Tarsnap Mastery — FreeBSD Mastery: ZFS
FreeBSD Mastery: Specialty Filesystems
FreeBSD Mastery: Advanced ZFS — PAM Mastery
Relayd and Httpd Mastery — Ed Mastery
FreeBSD Mastery: Jails — SNMP Mastery

The Networknomicon